The Destruction of a Continent

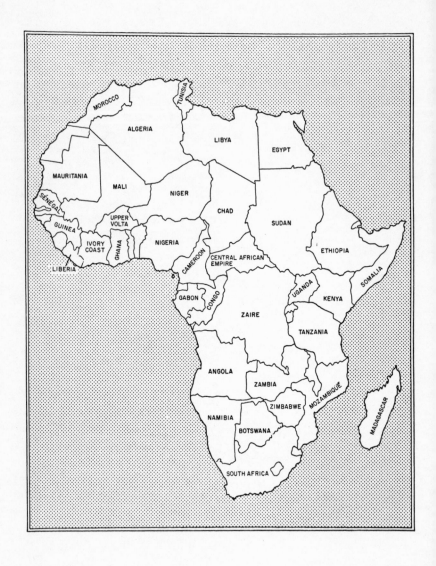

THE DESTRUCTION OF A CONTINENT / Africa and International Aid

Karl Borgin and Kathleen Corbett

Harcourt Brace Jovanovich, Publishers

San Diego   New York   London

Requests for permission to make copies
of any part of the work should be mailed to:
Permissions, Harcourt Brace Jovanovich, Publishers
757 Third Avenue, New York, N.Y. 10017.

Library of Congress Cataloging in Publication Data
Borgin, Karl.
The destruction of a continent.
1. Economic assistance—Africa.
2. Africa—Economic conditions—1960–
I. Corbett, Kathleen. II. Title.
HC800.B67   1982   338.91′096   82–47677
ISBN 0-15-125308-0   AACR2

Printed in the United States of America

First edition

B C D E

To our colleagues, friends, and students in Nairobi
who work so hard against great odds
to build a new and better Africa

Contents

ACKNOWLEDGMENTS   ix

INTRODUCTION   xi

1. The Scenario   3

2. From Vasco da Gama to Kurt Waldheim   12

3. The Last Invasion of Africa   25

4. The Aid Syndrome   46

5. The Failures   73

6. Science and Technology   99

7. Produce or Perish   126

8. The Obstacles   145

9. Maintaining the Illusion   164

10. Will Africa Survive?   179

    Epilogue   183

APPENDIX 1. Official Development Assistance
             from Six European and Two
             North American Donor
             Countries   189

APPENDIX 2. Growth Rate and Total Population
of Six Donor Countries in Europe
and Six Recipient Countries
in Africa   190

APPENDIX 3. Charts: 191
Population in 1980 and 2000
Annual Growth Rate 1960–70 and 1970–79
Food Production 1977–79
Aid Flow from OECD Countries
Future Increase of Aid

ACKNOWLEDGMENTS

The research for this book has been carried out over a period of many years in several African countries.

Information and data have been collected from numerous sources, among them local government offices, national and international aid organizations, several UN bodies and committees, and European and American embassies and consulates in the capitals of many African countries.

A source of sometimes quite intriguing information was the many conferences and meetings of African scientists, university lecturers, aid personnel, and UN staff from countries of widely different political and economic systems, such as Kenya, Nigeria, Ghana, Ethiopia, and Mozambique.

We are particularly grateful to colleagues and friends at Nairobi University for the numerous stimulating and frank discussions regarding the difficult problem of developing Africa.

Special thanks goes to Peter, in Kenya, who knows Africa better than most from colonial times to the present. His vast experience of Africa and access to reliable sources in central and eastern Africa were of great value during our research for the book.

We are also equally grateful to Elsie, in South Africa, for the enthusiastic help in sending us a constant stream of press cuttings and information over a period of many years.

Without the help and assistance we received from so many, it would have been impossible to compile the vast material required to study the complex problems of modern Africa and international aid.

Introduction

This book deals with a continent on its way either to a promising future or to total catastrophe.

In writing the book we have combined our knowledge and experience of the African continent, where we have worked and lived for more than twenty-five years. Karl Borgin, who is Norwegian, put his foot on African soil for the first time in 1954, after spending thirty-six hours on a SAS plane from New York to Nairobi, while Kathleen Corbett, who is British, arrived in South Africa a few years earlier.

In 1964 we met for the first time, and since then we have worked together doing research and teaching people in Africa, both black and white, in several parts of the continent. We have traveled extensively all over Africa, from Cape Town in the south to Cairo in the north. We have seen Africa under colonial rule; we have followed the decolonization of British, Portuguese, French, and Belgian territories in Africa; and we have witnessed the collapse of white rule in Angola, Mozambique, and Rhodesia.

We have lived and worked under white supremacy in South Africa and under independent black rule in eastern

Africa. We are probably two of a very few who have been employed first by a white university in South Africa and then by the most modern, and probably the best, university in independent black Africa, the University of Nairobi in Kenya.

We therefore have had many personal experiences, good and bad, from both black and white Africa. From contacts over many years with the numerous peoples living in Africa—blacks, Europeans, Asians, and those of mixed races—we feel we are able to understand Africa's problems without taking sides as to who is right and who is wrong.

From the Faculty of Science at Nairobi University, where Professor Borgin taught industrial chemistry, and the School of Journalism at the same university, where Mrs. Corbett taught photojournalism, we learned a lot about the scientific, technical, and human problems of modern black Africa. There we came to respect and admire the young generation of Africans who often worked so hard to get the qualifications they needed for guiding Africa toward a better future. In addition, we learned about their problems and the shortcomings of their politicians, who often were more interested in their own careers than in the future of their countries.

We are convinced that Africa has chosen the wrong models for development. Neither the Western form of a free-enterprise system, with its permanent economic crisis, unemployment, and increasing inflation, nor the socialist system, with a planned economy, collective farms, and suppression of the freedom of the individual, is the solution to Africa's problems.

Africa must free itself from models of development imported from overseas. It is not enough to abolish colonialism, which brought both good and bad to Africa. The systems imported from Europe must be dismantled and replaced with something the African, and only the African, can develop himself. If he fails, Africa, with its decreasing food production and rapidly increasing population, is doomed.

We do not offer any political solution to Africa's problems, for we do not believe the problems of development in Africa are of a political nature. We do not present any program for survival, which preoccupies so many leading politicians in the West and the Communist bloc, simply because there is no single program for survival. We do not invent grandiose schemes, which every meeting and conference of the UN and its international bureaucracy offer to Africa, because we know that no grandiose schemes conceived in Europe or the United States will ever work in Africa.

We do not believe in the type of political, academic, or theoretical research done on Africa in Europe or the U.S. We feel that the many publications appearing in the West and within the Communist bloc by self-appointed experts, who do not know and understand Africa, not only are misleading and wrong but can sometimes do considerable harm. The numerous solutions offered to Africa from outside the continent are so politically motivated and shrouded in political philosophy that they ignore the real problems and concentrate on theoretical, sometimes completely unrealistic solutions.

In the West, this type of activity has reached its peak, and we sincerely hope that it will never surpass the publication of the report of the so-called Independent Commission on International Development Issues and the announcement of a New International Economic Order. We will deal with both at some length, for we believe that if the West accepts the unrealistic recommendations of the commission and the political philosophy of the New International Economic Order, it will hasten the decline of modern Africa and contribute considerably to the final catastrophe.

While the West is engrossed in its plans for an ever-increasing aid to Africa as the only solution to development, it tends to forget that almost 30 percent of Africa's territory is occupied by ten socialist-oriented countries accounting for 25 percent of the continent's population. Africa experts from the Soviet Academy of Science and from other countries in the Communist bloc, such as Bulgaria, are extremely active in shaping their own Marxist solution to Africa's problems. After all, they have free access to almost one-third of Africa for whatever experiments they intend to carry out.

The solutions to Africa's problems as discussed in so many publications from Progress Publishing House and the Academy of Science, both in Moscow, are dangerous for the same reason the solutions recommended in the report of the Independent Commission and the New International Economic Order are dangerous. They are both politically motivated and ignore the needs of the Africans themselves.

In this book, we have tried to avoid all the pitfalls of political philosophy, dogmatic thinking, and economic theories so often advocated from the outside world. We try to see the problems from inside Africa, and after twenty-five years on the continent we hope we can see the problems as the Africans themselves do. With this in mind, we have presented our views on the development of Africa. We have avoided the phraseology of the Africa experts in Europe and the U.S. We have rejected the glamorous, grandiose schemes of the UN and its many organizations as unrealistic and hopeless. Instead we have accepted the hypothesis that we have to go back to basics, back to the very nature of the Africans and their continent.

We therefore have to accept that freedom, independence, and self-rule did not bring the happiness to Africa we all expected. We must not ignore the fact that from a reasonably well-organized colonial rule, Africa has entered a period of turmoil, violence, political suppression, and agricultural decline. Of all the problems, and they are all interrelated, we are convinced that the most serious one is the decline in agriculture in Africa. With less food available and a rapidly increasing population—one of the fastest-growing in the world—Africa is facing starvation on a scale we have never seen before. The solution to development in Africa is not to industrialize but to use the continent's gift, the millions of square kilometers of red, fertile soil. The Africans must preserve and develop their own agriculture, which has been the foundation for their very existence for thousands of years.

While the international community, the UN and its bureaucracy, and the national aid organizations all over the world hold their numerous conferences, table more resolutions, write more reports, and plan new projects, Africa is slowly disintegrating.

We are convinced the Africans must continue their own development according to their own timetable, their own skill and ability. They must follow their own dreams and desires, rejecting the program imposed by the international bureaucracy, which will desynchronize the development of the continent and disturb the ecological equilibrium it has taken millennia to establish. If the Africans fail in accepting that they, and they alone, can solve the development of their continent, no one can stop the impending catastrophe.

A Word on Language

The United Nations, foreign aid organizations, and the international bureaucracy have created in all spheres of their activities a large number of new terms. The real meaning of the terminology used at their numerous conferences and in their many publications is obscure to most and without precise definition even to the initiated. For anyone outside the huge international bureaucracy, it seems like a foreign language. This represents a problem in the writing of a book like this one on Africa and international aid.

After more than twenty years of indoctrination by

national and international aid organizations, a certain terminology has come into common use, and we have had to use it to some extent, even though the terms lack definition or represent a number of misconceptions and fallacies.

Some of the most basic concepts are without clear meaning or definition—for example, "developed" and "undeveloped," the "Third World," and the so-called North-South dialogue. A large portion of the terminology is created for propaganda purposes and does not represent real, concrete concepts. Many are misnomers, and much is pure fiction, like the term "Third World." The Third World is a myth. As the well-known expert on international aid, P. T. Bauer, expresses it: "Without foreign aid there is no Third World" (*Equality. The Third World: An Economic Delusion*, Weidenfeld and Nicolson, London, 1981).

Very often terms and concepts are purposely created without any clear definition. As we shall discuss later in the book, it is often convenient for the international bureaucracy to operate with terms no one really understands. It is a sort of planned confusion that can be exploited to the fullest for a variety of political motives.

The term "New International Economic Order" belongs to this category. Nobody really understands what the New International Economic Order is, but the United Nations, national and international aid organizations, and the international bureaucracy use the term a thousand times a day all over the world as a universal solution for anything from mass starvation to nuclear war. It is used simultaneously by the U.S.S.R. to promote world socialism, by the Scandinavian countries as a slogan for a world welfare state, and by countries in Africa and Asia as blackmail against the industrialized countries of the West.

Often sinister political motives are hidden behind apparently well-meaning slogans, of which the term "equitable distribution of wealth" is the one most used—or misused, depending upon one's understanding of another term, "global egalitarianism." No concept has been exploited to such an extent as that of redistributing wealth to create equality. And no concept contains such a potential threat to the free Western world as the harmful consequences of this international propaganda. We should, therefore, consider Milton Friedman's warning about the misuse of the concept of equality to be universally valid, not only within societies but among nations: "A world that puts equality—in the sense of equality of outcome—ahead of freedom, will end up with neither equality nor freedom" (*Free to Choose*, Harcourt Brace Jovanovich, New York, 1980).

In the following chapters we will discuss the terminology now internationally accepted and analyze the real significance and the propaganda value of those terms. We have to accept the use of some of them, albeit with our own definitions. In addition, we have created our own terms, not to add to the confusion, but to describe various aspects of international aid to Africa. When we refer to the administrators of the mammoth organizations of the United Nations and their many branches as "superbureaucrats," we do this simply because there is no other term that adequately characterizes the often anonymous men behind the most expensive, cumbersome, complicated, and powerful bureaucracy the world has ever known. When we refer to the promoters of international aid as the "aid fanatics," it is because there is no other appropriate term to describe those people who unreservedly believe in international aid as a sort of religion. As Crusaders for a New World Order, they are adamant that all problems of development can be overcome by confiscating the American and European taxpayers' money and sending a never-ending stream of billions of U.S. and Canadian dollars, German marks, English pounds, Scandinavian kroner, and Dutch gulden to disappear in Africa's hot deserts or steaming jungles.

To understand one another, whether we agree or not, depends to a large extent on the use of terminology that can be exactly defined. We have therefore tried to use a precise terminology, although often with a quite personal flavor, which we hope will appeal to some but be criticized by others. This is unavoidably the fate of a critical analysis such as ours of a world-wide problem to which there may be no solution.

The Destruction of a Continent

INTERNATIONAL AID WILL NEVER SUCCEED IN AFRICA BECAUSE:

1. The African population will increase from 450 to 900 million in twenty years.

2. In Kenya and Tanzania alone, with limited areas of arable land, the population will increase from 32.4 million to 61 million by the end of the century.

3. An additional 250 million will live in Africa's cities and towns by the year 2000 and will consume huge amounts of extra food without producing any agricultural crops in return.

4. Over a period of seven years, the food production in Africa dropped by ten percent.

5. Europe, already burdened with 25 million unemployed, cannot tax her own population further to provide aid to Africa's increasing urban population of 333 million by the year 2000.

6. Donor countries in Europe cannot maintain aid to countries in Africa where the rate of the population growth is more than seven times their own.

7. The huge transfer of resources to Africa creates conditions that require further aid in a never-ending vicious circle.

8. International aid accelerates a chain reaction with a built-in mechanism for its own destruction as the population explosion in Africa completely overtaxes the U.S. and Europe's capacity to satisfy the never-ending demands for more aid.

1 / The Scenario

It was Wednesday, which meant that we had no lectures to give at Nairobi University. It was the day we could use for research without being disturbed by administrative or teaching duties.

This Wednesday was different, however. We had gone to the Kenyatta Conference Center in Nairobi, where we had managed to get permits to follow one of the many conferences of the Organization of African Unity, the OAU, which for many years had been one of the most important of all the pan-African organizations.

In the huge, circular assembly hall of the Kenyatta Conference Center could be seen a cross section of Africa's almost 500 million people. There were practically no European or American faces. One could study a representative sampling of the African elite—those who ruled over the life and destiny of millions—from Mozambique, Zimbabwe, and Angola in the south, from the Arab countries in the north, from Liberia, Ghana, and Nigeria in the west, from Kenya, Ethiopia, and Somalia in the east.

The staff of the local broadcasting service, the Voice of Kenya, was busy testing their TV cameras and installing small floodlights at vantage points around the assembly hall. Some of those whom we knew waved to us and came over for a brief chat. Behind the glass cubicles for the interpreters, men and women were busy testing microphones, tape recorders, and amplifiers, and journalists and reporters from all over Africa were waiting for the meeting to start.

The big hall was filled with the sounds of a dozen African and Arab languages, and occasionally the lingua franca of the West Coast, French, could be heard, while the language of the last big imperialists, English, could be heard when the Bantus of the south tried to communicate with the Arabs of the north. We looked around to see who spoke with the unmistakable accent of South African English, and saw a typical Cape Colored, probably from the African National Congress of South Africa, engrossed in a long discussion with a tall Kikuyu, who answered him with the equally unmistakable accent of colonial English, which he had probably acquired during his early days at some British mission school.

Strategically positioned near the entrance to the huge hall were members of the political elite in Kenya welcoming all the African visitors. There was a lot of handshaking, backslapping, and big smiles as the ever smiling and smartly dressed Kenyans, in tailor-made English striped suits, recognized old friends and government representatives who had taken part in so many earlier OAU meetings in Africa's new and modern capitals.

Wherever we looked, we saw something new and different, a real cross section of Africa, people with different ethnic and racial backgrounds, of many religions and from widely different political systems: the usually arrogant Nigerians, dressed in long, flowing robes and odd colorful headgear, which to the initiated signaled the status and position of the representatives from the wealthiest state in black Africa; north African Arabs, with the chiseled, proud features of the desert Bedouin, who had changed their traditional gowns for business suits, designed and made not in London but in Paris; Ethiopians dressed in suits with an unmistakable East-European cut, which did not detract from the pharaohlike features of their slim, golden-brown faces; Muslims and Christians from Sudan, Chad, and Niger, where the animosity between them still could be sensed in spite of all the smiles and prolonged and constant handshaking; blacker than all the other black Africans, the central Africans and some of the west Africans in their long, usually white, traditional robes; the Angolans, still dressed with some of the elegance of their old colonial masters, some of them half-Portuguese themselves; the Mozambiquans, looking out of place with the drabness of Red China and East Germany combined, dressed as they were in badly made Mao-style uniforms or ill-fitting East-European suits.

The assembly hall was different that day from what we were used to from all the other meetings we had attended here. This was not one of the numerous United Nations conferences that went on all the time in Nairobi. This was a meeting of Africans only, for Africa, about Africa, and by Africans. Missing from the usual scene in Nairobi were the Americans in their checkered trousers, the British in their blazers and gray slacks, the pale Scandinavians in their immaculate safari suits, the ever efficient and correct Germans in equally correct attire, and the truculent, never-smiling Russian delegates in their overpadded, out-of-place, and incredibly old-fashioned suits. Also missing from the scene were the booming voices of American delegates, who normally could be heard from one end of the conference hall to the other. Neither could one hear the clipped speech of the British, the singsong of the Scandinavians, the precise, school-English of the Germans, the gritty, automatonlike English of the Russians, or the specially flavored English only a French delegate could speak.

With these thoughts in mind, we started to read some of the press releases that would appear in local newspapers all over Africa the next morning. There was suddenly a hushed silence, and the murmur of voices in the huge hall died down as the speakers and the chief delegates took their places at the rostrum.

The performance was impressive indeed. Africans are born speakers, and those here were the best of them all. They not only knew how to talk, they also knew how to argue and quarrel. After the usual denunciation of South Africa and Israel and the passage of resolutions condemning the Israelis' control of Jerusalem, they got down to the business of saving Africa from hunger, poverty, internal strife, revolution, and war. During the conference, which continued for several more days, nothing new was said, and the same old resolutions were adopted.

The very name of the organization, the Organization of African Unity, is a mockery, because there is really no unity about anything except that the South Africans and the Israelis are racists and represent a threat to international peace. That the Cuban troops in Angola, the invasion of Uganda by Tanzanian troops, and the Ethiopian military attacks on Somalia were a threat to the peace on the black continent was largely ignored, but it did at least give some of the delegates the opportunity for some quite formidable oral battles.

The conference soon turned into a meeting like so many others we had witnessed in Nairobi. It was turned into a battle between the delegates, who were all competing about presenting the most grandiose scheme for saving Africa. This was a conference about illusions that, with the exception of the young students who had managed to get entrance cards to the meeting, very few actually believed in. Whether or not the many resolutions could be carried out was of little consequence. What was important was to be quoted by the press and have one's speeches printed in the local newspaper when the delegates returned home.

We looked at the delegates, listened to their speeches, followed the discussions, and wondered all the time what the Africans congregated here really represented. Did they really represent the new Africa, the free, independent Africa, and a change from colonial rule to a new life for all?

They were well fed—in fact, we had never seen so many fat Africans in one place—luxuriously and expensively dressed, and outside a fleet of luxury cars was waiting to take them back to the Hilton, Intercontinental, and Norfolk hotels before they had to face the ardor of the cocktail parties and the nightlife of Nairobi. Most of them had one thing in common. They had come to power as the result of political intrigues, corruption, military coups, or brutal and total suppression of their political opponents in their own countries.

Here, right in the middle of Africa, in the capital of the country that had produced the greatest black statesman on the continent, Jomo Kenyatta, here in the great hall of the conference center that bears his name, the new African elite had come together, representing not the *people* of their countries but a new power structure not much different from the old colonial rule except for the substitution of black faces for white ones. Looking at the elegantly dressed delegates, it was inevitable to compare them with the tens of thousands of poor Africans in the slums of Nairobi, the hundreds of thousands without jobs, and the many students without any work for which we had trained them.

Was this the Africa the Africans really wanted? Did the bombastic speeches concern the real Africa? Did the elite inside the conference center still believe they represented the millions outside, and did those who had no say still believe the elite represented them?

We doubted it. In spite of the impressive promises given at every conference in Africa, the mutual trust was not there any more. Africans had come to realize that the new elite was far removed from the realities of modern Africa. The intellectual Africans in particular looked upon the summit meeting of the OAU as just another expensive gathering of Africa's new rulers who believed the future could be changed by passing new resolutions and publishing impressive statements.

When the conference was over and the flood of resolutions had been dispatched to the various parts of the world, nothing had changed. The only decision that would be followed up was the one recommending the time and place for still another OAU meeting in another impressive conference hall in another of Africa's capitals.

The whole exercise we had witnessed that day symbolizes the inability of Africa's new leaders to live up to expectations and to understand the hopes and aspirations of the millions they rule and govern. Africa's elite, as is so clearly demonstrated by meetings of the kind we had been attending, have simply taken over the role of their old masters, the colonials, and have, in addition, acquired all the characteristics of the most inefficient, garrulous, money-spending, and pompous bureaucracy the world has ever known: the United Nations, with all its international organizations, committees, meetings, and enormous administrative apparatus. It is the same everywhere—in Lagos, Accra, Abidjan, Freetown, Monrovia, Addis Ababa, Kampala, Dar es Salaam, and Lusaka. Here was Africa's problem in a nutshell: the vociferous elite, whose inability to act will bring them into confrontation with the millions who have little opportunity to be heard but possess a burning desire to act.

When we left the conference building and strolled across the large, sunny square with a stone statue of Jomo Kenyatta, we agreed about one thing: the African elite certainly had been able to imitate exactly their counterparts in Europe, the U.S., and the United Nations. Like politicians in the West, and like members of the huge international bureaucracy working within the many UN organizations, they could talk, discuss, argue, and promise for days and in the end accomplish little or nothing.

How different the men and women must have been who a hundred years ago had walked across the swampy fields or had ridden up dusty Government Road after the Mombasa-Uganda railway had given the impetus for building the railway town in the middle of nowhere that is now Nairobi. As we walked up Government Road to reach our car, parked on the university campus near the Norfolk Hotel, it was almost impossible not to think about those who started it all, the people who really built up the continent and founded everything upon which modern Africa is based: Lord Delamere, who in 1897 came to what is now Kenya after walking through 1600 kilometers of African wilderness from Somalia; Frederick Lugard, who in 1891 entered east Africa after marching a small contingent of soldiers from the Congo to Uganda; and George Whitehouse, who in 1895 left the small S.S. *Ethiopia* in the old Arab harbor near Fort Jesus in Mombasa to take charge of the most enterprising, and probably the craziest, railway ever built in Africa or anywhere else.

Using modern terminology, Lord Delamere would have been the agricultural expert, Lugard would have been the administrator or project planner, and Whitehouse, the technologist.

Without men like Lord Delamere, Lugard, and Whitehouse, there would have been no Nairobi, there would have been no Kenyatta Conference Center, and there would have been no blacks at the conference center condemning the old colonials, who, in fact, had made the Africans' present way of life possible.

Lord Delamere personified the type of men who *settled* in Africa and were responsible for introducing the continent to modern agriculture. Lugard introduced a type of administration and government, which the black, whether he likes it or not, has made his own. Whitehouse introduced Africa to modern technology on a scale hitherto unknown.

They, and men like them, did the job for everyone to see, even today, almost 100 years later.

Deep in thought and sometimes involved in long discussions about Africa, we finally reached the university and decided to have some ice-cold fruit juice at the Norfolk. We found a table on the open veranda, where Lord Delamere's name was chiseled into a plaque near the bar and where the old colonials, the famous explorers, the well-known politicians, the big-game hunters, and the officers of east Africa's famous military units, like the KAR and EAMR, had enjoyed a sundowner and discussed the future of Africa.

The scene was, however, as different as it could be from the days of the colonials and the settlers. Gone were the men of vision, inspiration, and courage. Gone were the men who really *believed* in Africa and devoted their lives to the continent. Around us could be heard the Europeans and Americans on organized photo safaris, with international aid organizations, or from the numerous embassies and consulates in Nairobi.

What made men like Lord Delamere, Lugard, and Whitehouse so different from all those spending their time in east Africa today was that the first settlers devoted their lives—in fact, gave their lives—to the future of Africa. Those present that day—lounging in their imported safari suits, walking around in blue jeans, or sweating in their uncomfortable, hot business suits, depending upon which category they represented—would never be able to do what the previous generation of white men and women had accomplished in Africa. They were people with no imagination, of little courage, and devoid of inspiration. They were building a piece of Europe in Africa under the slogan of aid and development and had changed the new Nairobi into an image of Europe and the U.S.

Opposite the Norfolk Hotel, one could hear the hustle and bustle as the students went to their classes. Maybe there, out there among the groups of talkative students, inside the lecture rooms, or behind the laboratory benches, were those who would build a new and better Africa. This is Africa's only hope, because one thing is clear: the African elite we had left an hour earlier at the Kenyatta Conference Center, and the Europeans and Americans surrounding us on the Norfolk terrace, would never accomplish what they had promised and talked about for years. They were not the *doers* of yesterday but the *talkers* of today.

It is now up to the Africans. The scenario is vast, the actors many, and the prospects alarming. How alarming, we shall outline in the following chapters.

2 / From Vasco da Gama to Kurt Waldheim

The Early Seafarers

Man has perhaps lived in Africa as long as on any other continent. Some even believe that our hominid ancestors developed to *Homo sapiens* on the black continent and populated the rest of the world from there, while others are convinced that the people of Africa came from the Eurasian continent and crossed the Sahara to settle in what must have been the most fertile continent on earth.

We may never know for certain if man invaded Africa or developed there, but we are reasonably certain that 50,000 years ago a population emerged who had learned to make fire, use tools, and protect themselves in caves and roofed shelters.

Africa, like most other continents, went through the various stone ages, and 40,000 years before our time Africa was populated by people who showed major regional variations. Soon after 10,000 B.C. *Homo sapiens* in one form or another was predominant everywhere.

At some time many thousands of years ago, the climate of the Sahara grew cooler and less dry. The land became fertile, pastures appeared, and the country was crisscrossed with rivers. Between 4000 and 3000 B.C., one of man's most spectacular civilizations developed in the Nile Valley and based its progress on its ability to grow food by systematic agriculture, sowing, and irrigation. This people, who came from across the Sinai Peninsula, produced a race in the Nile Valley that in the relatively short span of two thousand years accomplished more than the rest of Africa had managed ever before. The first contacts with European civilizations were with the Phoenicians, Greeks, and Romans, who occupied, conquered, and settled in North Africa. With the invention of the ship, the seas ceased to be a barrier to man and became his highway, his transport system, and a highly efficient method of communication. From 1200 to 146 B.C. the masters of trade, exploration, and communication were the people of the sea, the Phoenicians, who spread out from the coastal cities of what is today Lebanon to tie together Europe, the Middle East, and North Africa with a network of sea routes. At that time, however, the Sahara was once more becoming drier and again severed the northern part of Africa and the rest of the continent. North Africa became part of Europe, and the magnificent ruins of the Roman cities of Leptis Magna, Dougga, and Carthage tell a story not about Africa but about Europe. Those who are fortunate enough, once in their lifetime, to have sought shelter under what is left of the splendid arches of the beautiful Roman villa at Utica in Tunisia are almost painfully aware that this cool oasis in the hot, dusty, and backward country was once part of Europe and almost completely isolated from black Africa.

The Phoenicians were probably the first to sail down the coast of Africa, but how far they really came we do not know. Africa was discovered not by exploration across Africa, through the inhospitable Sahara Desert, but by exploration around Africa in an effort to reach India and the Far East. What opened up Africa to the Europeans after the collapse of the Roman empire and the withdrawal of the Europeans from North Africa was the ingenuity, the inventiveness, the desire to learn more about the world, the urge to explore, and—maybe even more—the courage of a small nation in Europe, Portugal. The Portuguese sent their superb sailing ships, the caravels, into the unknown to find an entirely new world.

In 1416, on the eve of what later became known as the great age of discovery, Prince Henry of Portugal established a school of navigation at Sagres near Cape St. Vincent. A scholar, scientist, soldier, and crusader, he became obsessed with his expeditions and voyages into the unknown. Under Prince Henry, Portuguese trade expanded tremendously, and his brave captains ventured farther and farther down the coast of Africa.

The first to reach the southernmost tip of Africa was Bartholomew Diaz, who in 1487 discovered what later became known as the Cape of Good Hope. Unfortunately, Prince Henry did not live to hear about the triumphs of Portuguese seamanship and how one of the most outstanding of all explorers, Vasco da Gama, rounded the Cape of Good Hope in 1497 and was able to circumnavigate the whole of Africa and reach what later became Mozambique and Mombasa.

The daring Portuguese expeditions opened up the sea route around Africa to others, and soon other enterprising mariners, the British and the Dutch, followed where the Portuguese had been the pioneers.

The mastery of the sea routes made the Europeans the most mobile people in the world, and they took full advantage of their skill and experience to be the great conquerors of the world. One of the continents they conquered was Africa.

The first English voyage around the Cape of Good Hope, along the Portuguese-controlled route, was under James Lancaster in 1591. Holland was, however, for many years in the lead, and sent a total of fifteen expeditions around Africa between 1595 and 1601. The main target for their trade and expansion was, however, not Africa, which they had to circumnavigate, but India and the Far East, which resulted in the formation of the Dutch East India Company in 1602 and the granting of a royal charter by Queen Elizabeth I to the English East India Company about the same time.

The real exploration of Africa could not take place as long as access to the continent was confined to coastal towns and supply stations serving their ships on their way to India and the Far East. Occasionally where one could find navigable rivers, the country was explored a few miles inland, but the interior of the huge continent remained almost totally unknown. To penetrate the dark unknown was a challenge that was soon to be taken up by another breed of men, the explorers, who came mainly from countries like England, Germany, and France.

The Explorers

Perhaps more than any other, the British are a race of explorers and adventurers, and late in the eighteenth century they embarked upon an organized exploration of the interior of Africa. The African Association, the fore-runner of the Royal Geographical Society of London, was founded in 1788 to promote exploration of Africa, with a clear second objective of advancing British trade and gaining practical authority of the unknown continent. In 1795, the association sent a very enthusiastic and able volunteer, a young Scottish doctor, Mungo Park, on an expedition to explore the River Niger. Dr. Park's journeys during 1795–97 into the western Sudan heralded the period of the bravest men of all, the explorers.

These brave men were all exposed to the same dangers: tropical climates, ranging from extreme dryness to choking humidity; temperatures changing from unbearable heat to freezing cold; diseases varying from permanent fevers to fatal dysenteries and never-healing sores; wild animals harassing the expeditions or killing their members; insects making life unbearable and spreading deadly diseases;

poisonous snakes killing swiftly or paralyzing the unfortunate victim; hostile natives attacking the expeditions, killing their members and stopping all progress into the interior.

In spite of all the odds against them, there was no lack of enthusiasm and support for the expeditions, nor was there any shortage of able and courageous volunteers, who often were men trained in science and medicine. There were also men of faith, often having medical skills, like the most famous of them all, David Livingstone, missionary, medical doctor, and explorer. This was likewise the era of the naturalists, a unique breed, now extinct, who were versed in a number of physical, chemical, and biological sciences and who left their dusty laboratories and old universities in the United Kingdom, Germany, and France to find honor and glory, but who often met with sudden death in Africa's sweltering jungles or deserts.

This was also the era of the missionaries. Members of the new and the old missionary societies, like the London Missionary Society and the British Church Missionary Society, not only preached the gospel and played an important role in opening up the dark continent; they were the first to be genuinely interested in the *people* of Africa as well as the geography and plant and animal life. Some succeeded, others became famous, while many were buried before they had walked a few miles into the mysterious but dangerous continent.

From the beginning, the great explorers seemed to be obsessed by rivers, where they came from and where they finally reached the estuary on some unknown coast. Names like Niger, Nile, Zambezi, and Congo are associated with almost all the early explorers.

After Mungo Park's expeditions into the western Sudan, the French explorer René Caillié also tried to follow the River Niger, walking through the Sudan and Sahara after stopping over in Timbuktu, and finally reaching Morocco during 1828.

By 1860 the main features of the western African interior

were known. Many other explorers had concentrated their efforts in eastern Africa to find the sources of the Nile, while still others were more interested in central and southern Africa and in the Congo and Zambezi rivers. Probably the most remarkable of them all was David Livingstone, who embarked on a series of expeditions in 1841, which he heroically continued for a quarter of a century and which took him all over Africa.

In 1857 Richard Burton and his friend John Speke walked thousands of miles in the east African hinterland and, among many other places, discovered Lake Tanganyika in 1858. Speke later continued alone to find Lake Victoria, and then, with another friend and explorer, James Grant, he finally reached the upper waters of the White Nile.

One of the greatest scientific explorers was the German Heinrich Barth, who during several expeditions between 1844 and 1855 discovered the exact course of the River Niger. An equally well known countryman of Barth's was Georg Schweinfurth, who in 1868–71 explored the watersheds of the White Nile.

Some of the most dramatic ventures, well known to most of us, were the journeys of Henry M. Stanley and his Anglo-American expedition during 1874–77. With the American flair for publicity and grandiose schemes, Stanley set out as "Commander" of the New York *Herald* Expedition to find Doctor Livingstone, who at that time was considered missing in the dark continent.

That he finally found Livingstone, lost in thousands and thousands of square kilometers of unknown jungle and desert, must be one of the miracles of the world, but that during the search he also became one of the great explorers of Africa is due to his persistence, love of adventure, and his incredible ability to quickly organize a type of expedition of which he had no prior experience.

By the 1880s, the African interior and the unknown hinterlands were explored in all directions. The last of the great explorers, Joseph Thompson, from Edinburgh University, was like so many others a naturalist, and he wandered all over east Africa, to Kenya, Uganda, and the Great Rift Valley, and even explored all the way down to South Africa. Well before the beginning of the twentieth century, Africa was no longer the dark, unknown continent, but the lure of Africa still remained. The explorers had done their heroic job, and now other pioneers, the colonials and the settlers, were preparing for their contribution to the opening up of the African continent.

The Colonials and the Settlers

While the impact of Africa on Europe and America had been enormous, causing tremendous interest in the huge continent, the impact of Europe and America on Africa was for all practical purposes negligible or nonexistent until the end of the nineteenth century.

If our contact with Africa had ended with the great explorers, Africa would have continued to exist as it had for tens of thousands of years. Park, Caillié, Livingstone, Burton, Speke, Grant, Barth, Schweinfurth, Stanley, and Thompson would soon have been forgotten, and as far as Africa was concerned, they might well have never existed. While the explorers had been few indeed, it was the development of industry and commerce in Europe that made it possible to send to the new continent men and women who went not only to explore but to stay and make Africa their new home.

The invention of the steam engine and the resulting greater mobility of men, raw materials, food, and finished products signaled the next phase in the Europeans' conquest of Africa. Rivalry, the competition among the great powers, dreams of world conquest, none of these made the scramble for Africa a reality. It was, rather, the development of a new technology that made it possible, whether desirable or not, to get to Africa and stay there.

It seemed that nobody "owned" Africa. The Africans themselves were completely ignored, and the struggle among the European powers for possession of Africa's land soon led to the colonial partition of virtually the entire continent. What the well-known historian and expert on Africa Basil Davidson called the invasion of Africa took place during a relatively short period, between 1880 and 1900. This says a lot for the tremendous reserves of energy, drive, and industriousness of Europeans, their highly developed technological skill at the end of the last century, and their superb ability to organize and administer. That a few European powers were able to carve up the continent, establish borders, and institute colonial rules in the short period of about twenty years is remarkable.

From 1900 to 1920, most of Africa was ruled by countries already established as imperial powers of long standing, like England and Portugal, and by the newcomers in the field, like France, Germany, and Belgium.

Africa became divided into major areas based on the country in Europe that was to be their colonial master. The largest areas belonged to the British, who ruled Africa from the extreme south to the shores of the Mediterranean; to the French, who established a new colonial empire mainly in the west and the north; to the Portuguese, who had taken out large slices of Africa in Mozambique and Angola; to the Belgians, who to their own surprise had acquired the whole of the Congo; to the Germans, who desperately wanted to convince themselves that they also could be a colonial power; and to the Italians, who hoped to restore their imperial past. The colonial period, which for the Germans was painfully concluded with the loss of their colonies after the First World War, lasted up to 1945 and a few years later, until the whole system started to disintegrate around 1960.

What is important for the present study, and vitally important for the future of Africa, is the tremendous impact of the short colonial rule on the development of the African continent. During a brief period—so short, in fact, in historical perspective that it could with justification be called Africa's colonial interlude—Africa and the Africans were rudely brought into contact with a civilization, cultures, religions, science, and technology that were not only new and different but entirely alien and even hostile to the kind of people who lived on this vast continent. The impact was shattering and often devastating. After the colonial interlude, Africa would never be the same again, and the good and bad of colonial rule will have an everlasting effect.

While the early explorers had been only observers of Africa, the colonials and the settlers who swarmed over Africa, from south to north and west to east, wanted to change Africa into a part of their countries of origin.

The classic colonials were the British, whom other European powers tried in vain to copy or imitate. These unique people, whom Churchill often referred to as the Island Race, combined all the virtues and vices on which empires have been based. From their Colonial Office in London they sent excellent administrators, without whom no colony could function; from Sandhurst and other military schools they sent superb officers, without whom the empire could not be defended; and from all over the British Isles they sent young men and women, the settlers, without whom they could never hope to build up agriculture and industries in their African colonies. But with all this they made the fatal mistake of regarding all colonial peoples as second-class citizens in their own homelands.

Spearheading this invasion were the dreamers, the visionaries, and those who wanted to conquer for the sake of conquering, to rule for the sake of ruling, the true imperialists like Sir Cecil Rhodes, Lord Salisbury, General Gordon, Lord Walseley, Herbert Kitchener, Frederick Lugard, and many others.

England dreamed about Pax Britannica, and ruled her colonies and possessions in Africa as the Persians, the Greeks, and the Romans had ruled before them. They committed the same crimes and made the same blunders as any other empire, but they excelled in heroic deeds, endless toil, hard work, and constructive undertakings. They transformed the continent, revolutionizing African agriculture, building a network of roads and railways, and bringing an orderly administration where there had been none before.

While the early mariners and the first explorers left Europe in search of the unknown, while the colonial administrators and imperial officers spent their years in Africa on behalf of their glorious fatherland, the settlers, unlike all the others, came to Africa to stay. The Dutch and British in South Africa, the Portuguese in Mozambique and Angola, the Belgians in the Congo, the French in northern and central Africa, and the British in Kenya, Uganda, and Rhodesia—all came to make Africa their own country, their new home, and a land where they could bring up their children.

The settlers, more than any other group, were responsible for the impact of Europe upon Africa. They were also more responsible for creating a conflict between black and white in Africa than the colonial administrators and the military rulers.

The settlers suffered more tragedies than any other group when colonial rule later broke down and chaos, strife, and lawlessness followed. They, more than anyone else, were responsible for building up a new Africa, of which the building of a one-thousand-kilometer-long railway from Mombasa to the interior of Kenya and Uganda is an epic example. And they, more than anyone else, had more to lose when the colonial interlude came to an end.

The Demolishers

Those who build empires always believe they will last forever. The Persians and the Romans built their roads, irrigation systems, and majestic buildings to last for thousands of years. And the British built their imperial cities in almost every continent as monuments to their faith in the future.

But nothing lasts forever, and all empires have a built-in mechanism for their own destruction. After periods of expansion and conquest, building and organization are followed by decay and disintegration. Like huge biochemical processes consuming the components that keep them alive, empires exhaust themselves, wither, and die. Empires can die a natural death, as when the Persian and Roman empires crumbled from within. Empires can be conquered and disintegrate under sword and fire. They can also fall apart because the men who possess the rare combination of vision, will power, and skill upon which all empires are built, are gone.

But when the African colonies were dismantled and demolished, it was due to neither exhaustion nor conquest. It was due to neither rivalry between the colonial powers nor any decline in their military and industrial powers. The African colonies were demolished not by the Africans themselves, as many believe, but by the colonial powers themselves when they were still building a new world in Africa. The African colonists were destroyed at the peak of their development by a new breed of men and women, different from anyone the world had ever seen before. They were the crusaders for a new world free of imperialism and exploitation. They did what no one did before: they turned against their own kind.

They indoctrinated a whole generation of Africans, who went to Europe to study, about the evils of capitalism. They taught the Africans to hate the whites, and encouraged them to take up arms and destroy the colonials' empires in Africa. Intoxicated by the preachings of Marx and Lenin, Africans mobilized all their forces to demolish a world they had learned to hate and despise. With the same energy the colonial powers had devoted to build a new Africa, they set about tearing apart all that the colonials had accomplished. Under pressure from the United Nations, exposed to a relentless propaganda from the socialist movements in Eastern Europe, England, Germany, Holland, and Scandinavia, and confronted by guerrilla warfare and open hostilities, the colonial powers were eventually forced to dismantle and leave their colonial empires they so painstakingly had built up in Africa.

The rapid decolonization of Africa has been, and still is, a traumatic experience for the continent's own black population as well as the millions of white settlers, immigrants, and colonials who were uprooted, displaced, and forced to leave the parts of Africa they had built up and believed to be their own. That the well-organized colonial administration was often replaced by total chaos, and that the relatively peaceful conditions under colonial rule were replaced by unrest, revolutions, and civil wars, were of little consequence for those who at any price wanted to wreck colonial rule in Africa. The price was high, and the continent was swept by racial wars in North Africa, the Congo, Mozambique, Angola, and Rhodesia; savage civil wars in Nigeria, the Congo, Somalia, and Chad; and military invasion by Tanzania into Uganda, Ethiopia into Somalia, and Libya into Chad.

The key figure in the decolonization of Africa was Kurt Waldheim, secretary-general of the United Nations from 1972 to 1982, who demonstrated the same enthusiasm in tearing down the colonial system as the settlers had shown in building it up.

Flirting with any pro-Marxist organization in Africa, like SWAPO in Namibia, and always recognizing any terrorist organizations fighting against colonial rule, like the liberation movements of Angola, Mozambique, Guinea Bissau, and Cape Verde, Kurt Waldheim is unique in the history of Western civilization as the only man with high position and power—and he had plenty of both—who consequently and with great vigor supported any struggle, whether military, political, or economic, against his own kind, the European communities in Africa.

It is symbolic that when Kurt Waldheim addressed the OAU meeting in Addis Ababa in 1973, not a single word was said to praise what the white man had done in Africa during the last 300 years, but assurances were given to continue the efforts to decolonize Africa and to "liberate" the territories still ruled by white minorities.

The United Nations is also unique in being the only known large-scale international organization that took part in dismantling and demolishing the economic, political, and social systems of most of the continent without trying to substitute it with anything else. The last invaders of Africa—the United Nations and the international bureaucracy—represent a system that has built nothing to replace what they so effectively have helped to destroy.

The road from Vasco da Gama to Kurt Waldheim has been a long and difficult one. What started as an era of accomplishment and continued as an age of building and construction, has ended as a period of disintegration and chaos.

3 / The Last Invasion of Africa

For ten thousand years Africa developed naturally and established economic, political, and cultural systems that worked reasonably well. The thousands of tribes, ethnic groups, and peoples of various backgrounds had established an equilibrium with the surroundings and a balance between development and environment.

For a relatively short period of a few hundred years, Africa became the battleground for the imperial powers of Europe, and the continent was carved into colonies with very little regard for the Africans themselves. The colonial period brought to Africa European civilization, culture, administration, political systems, and technology. The colonials shook the foundations on which Africa had been based for thousands of years and changed Africa, for better and for worse, for all time to come. When the colonials left, a new group took over and tried to fill the vacuum left by the big powers of Europe: the international bureaucracy of the United Nations and a multitude of international and national aid organizations. They created a new concept —that of the underdeveloped nations of Africa—which the international bureaucracy set out to change practically overnight.

The concept of "underdeveloped," which is a stinging insult to Africa and to Africans, is totally meaningless, for there is no yardstick or parameter for development. When our forefathers in northern Europe were savages, clad in bearskins and hiding in deep forests, the city-states of Mesopotamia had developed societies that in some respects were superior to those of the modern world. When the flourishing cultures of Mesopotamia and other areas in the Middle East collapsed and vanished, the barbarians of northern Europe had only begun to organize themselves into nations that would later develop the technology upon which the whole modern world is based.

Four thousand years elapsed between the time Babylon and Nineveh were the cultural centers of the world and the day we landed men on the moon. Once the Assyrians, the Sumerians, and the Babylonians were the most advanced people on our planet. Today, the descendants of these once so proud and able people live in misery in the land between the Euphrates and the Tigris, while we rule supreme in technological achievements.

Who is developed and who is underdeveloped is therefore a question of time. We are all developed according to the circumstances under which we live. To label the Africans underdeveloped is an insult to their intelligence. Africans require only time.

Instead, the new breed of humanity who has invaded Africa is not prepared to give the Africans what they need most: *time*. They swarm in from the world's international airports to occupy the luxury hotels in Nairobi, Dar es Salaam, Lusaka, and most of Africa's capitals. They do not ask questions. They tell the Africans what is best for them. They established themselves everywhere, installing themselves in expensive offices, expanding their embassies, and building enormously expensive headquarters crawling with bureaucrats from all over the world. They are the members of the new international and national aid organizations and representatives from the numerous organizations of the United Nations.

On average, they know nothing about Africa, but they are more bombastic, more self-assured, and more high-handed than any colonial had ever been. They know everything, and no one else counts. They try desperately to compress technological development into a few years, a feat the colonial powers never attempted and which in other countries has taken thousands of years. They are obsessed by a ruthless determination and grand visions of turning Africa into a modern Europe or America. Disregarding all the experience gained during several centuries of colonial rule, they want to change Africa to fit an image conceived in the conference halls of the United Nations.

With the tremendous resources originating from the European and American taxpayers, they go about their work without taking advice from the Africans themselves or listening to the Europeans who lived and worked there for generations. Without the slightest hesitation they embark on programs that they believe will lead the Africans to the Promised Land. They ignore the most elementary and the most basic questions: does the African really want this type of development, and is he and his society really capable of transforming Africa to an image of the white man's idea of a perfect society?

The last invaders, the international bureaucrats, never stop to ask this question. They are all obsessed with one single myth: that Africa will develop according to their plan as long as international aid continues to pour billions into the black continent. This is the very foundation for the existence of the international bureaucrats. They therefore maintain this myth and refrain from asking difficult questions in order to preserve their own highly paid jobs within the international bureaucracy and because this is an official policy imposed on them from offices at home. Behind them in the UN and the departments of national governments in

Europe and America are men and women in influential positions for whom the Africans mean nothing but for whom the continent is a place where they can experiment with their political philosophies and ideas of new international, social, and economic systems. The humanitarian element of international aid is, contrary to what they want us to believe, of little importance. The most important aspects of international aid to Africa are mainly political, economic, and often military.

To understand the very nature of international aid, it is important to understand the type of men and women behind the huge aid organizations, to interpret the function of their operations, and to be aware of their motives. Who are these people coming to Africa as experts on aid and development? Who are these people who are convinced that only they have the recipe for successful development, who announce without hesitation to the whole world that they have found a program for survival? Who are these people who use a considerable part of their energies in impressing themselves and others about their own importance, and even refer to themselves as the world's most eminent and prominent people? Who are these people who unashamedly establish a UN Group of Eminent Persons as a sort of superspecimen of *Homo sapiens* and therefore claim a sort of monopoly on what they refer to as high-level talks on the problems of international aid? Where do these people come from, and what do they actually do in drawing up dozens of programs for saving the underdeveloped world?

They certainly are a breed we have never seen before —not that they never existed, but before the new international bureaucracy was established, they spent their lives as civil servants in obscure government departments scattered all over the world.

Practically all the senior staff members who run the various aid organizations or are attached to overseas embassies and consulates are recruited from the national bureaucracy of their country of origin. The overwhelming majority who join the international bureaucracy are bureaucrats already. They simply move from a national organization to an international one. Thus, the world becomes their arena. While their sphere was previously limited, now the world is their playground.

There is no limit to their grandiose thinking, but unfortunately their self-confidence is not a reflection of their skill, wisdom, and experience, and never before in the history of human society have there been so many people doing the wrong job at the wrong place and at the wrong time.

The primary reasons for this unsatisfactory situation within the international bureaucracy are as follows:

- There are seldom clear specifications or definitions of the jobs to be carried out,
- There are no rigid qualifications laid down for the holder of the various positions, and
- There are no measures for success or failure.

Of these, the most serious is the inability to evaluate the overall work of international organizations and the results of their projects. Never before has it been possible to engage thousands of people and spend billions of dollars and not be in the position to demonstrate or prove success. When the old settlers or colonials in Africa failed in growing food, establishing plantations, or building new transport systems, the failure was there for everyone to see. The European settlers in Africa *had* to succeed; otherwise they were finished, one way or the other.

Not so with those engaged in international aid. Although no one else outside their organizations can establish with any certainty exactly what they are engaged in, they themselves are convinced that whatever they do is a success, for the only thing they are engaged in is planning new meetings, giving speeches, taking part in discussions, and preparing new resolutions.

Being bureaucrats, first on a national level, then on an international level, they are convinced that all their work is a success. They do not acknowledge the concept of failure simply because in their type of work there is no failure. Their function, and the only work they know, is to spend, one way or another, millions upon millions of dollars of taxpayers' money.

In any private undertaking, the idea of success or failure is not theoretical but very real. One manufactures enough products, or grows enough food, to make a profit. If one fails in this, one has demonstrated an inability to operate successfully, and one is fired, or the company goes bankrupt, or both. But for the international bureaucracy failure does not mean an end to their activities or a total reorganization. If there should be the slightest doubt that they are not successful, they merely plan more meetings, give longer speeches, pass more resolutions, and publish more impressive reports.

Africans themselves are fully aware that national and international aid organizations and the various organizations belonging to the UN are staffed with useless, ignorant —ignorant about Africa, that is—and incompetent bureaucrats. What Africans, especially the intellectual Africans, say among themselves and to the few Europeans they take into their confidence is entirely different from what they say in speeches about the generous help from overseas without which agriculture and industry cannot be developed. In one way they could not care who these international bureaucrats are as long as the millions keep on coming in from overseas taxpayers.

In most cases their political views are those of the government, which means in practice that the staff of aid organizations from Norway, Sweden, Denmark, Germany, Holland, and to a lesser degree England are socialists and have been recruited under the social democratic governments in the Scandinavian and Continental countries and the Labour government in England. All are obsessed with the idea of transferring resources from the industrialized countries to Africa, and they are fanatical adherents to the concept of a New International Economic Order. It is almost impossible to find a single senior staff member who is critical about the work of the international bureaucracy or expresses any doubt that they, and only they, can save Africa.

The only aid organizations that are different are the French and American. The French gives aid to Africa from a simple and practical motivation: that aid in the long run will improve trade between France and her former colonies. The Americans do not suffer from the political ideologies of the countries in northern Europe, nor can they, as the French, try to improve trade with some former colonies. The Americans suffer from the misconception that they can buy friends and political influence by giving out millions of dollars for development—a system that either does not work or produces even the opposite effect.

The Communist bloc is in a peculiar position, and looks upon international aid as "a major instrument of imperialism's neocolonial policy" *(Neocolonialism and Africa*, Progress Publishers, Moscow, 1978), a sort of secret weapon in the same category as "the bourgeoisie's striving to use more camouflaged forms of exploitation and oppression of the working people" (Leonid Brezhnev, to the Twenty-fourth Congress of the Communist Party of the U.S.S.R., in Moscow, 1971). On the other hand, while international aid is condemned by the Communist bloc, they are quite enthusiastic about the latest philosophy about aid—the new international economic order—which they believe "will deal a telling blow to the policy of neocolonialism and in a large measure facilitate the solution of the vital problems of Africa (*Present-Day Development of Africa*, U.S.S.R. Academy of Sciences, Moscow, 1980).

Among the experts of foreign policy in the U.S.S.R., who are burdened with Lenin's anachronistic theories about imperialism, there seems to be agreement about the futility of foreign aid, for the U.S.S.R. has never been able to buy a real friend with money, as the painful experiences in Ethiopia, Sudan, and Somalia have taught them. Their enthusiasm for the new international economic order is based on the fact that it will cost the U.S.S.R. nothing but can be used as an instrument for spreading international socialism.

Aid Fanatics and Superbureaucrats

There are several categories of people who are engaged in international aid and the study of the African continent. The two most important are the aid fanatics, those who believe implicitly and without reservation in the value of aid to Africa, and the superbureaucrats, who are heads of the large UN organizations in various parts of the world.

The aid fanatics are actively engaged in the field or are working in offices of international and national aid organizations in Europe and the United States. Quite a number are employed by universities, research organizations, and Africa institutes in many countries. Research institutes of this kind are found almost anywhere, and to have an Africa institute of some sort becomes a question of prestige; even the Soviet Academy of Science has an Africa Institute in Moscow. The aid fanatics do at least believe in their work. On the other hand, the superbureaucrats are appointed to their positions not because they believe in aid or because they are interested in Africa but simply because they are national candidates proposed by member countries for important UN positions. The aid fanatics are found everywhere, but the superbureaucrats are found only within the UN and the international aid organizations. Sometimes the two types are combined in one, in which case we have a rare specimen with considerable power and authority. There are also the experts, the real ones and the self-appointed ones, whose interest in Africa may be of a practical nature or whose interest in Africa may be purely academic.

The aid fanatics, the superbureaucrats, and the experts may be different from one another, but they have one thing in common: they write articles and reports, pamphlets and books. The keenest ones and the really enthusiastic ones write many books, and there is no better way to find out about them than by studying the backgrounds, qualifications, and professional positions of the authors of the many books that have been recently published on international aid and Africa.

There is a striking similarity among the contributors of some representative books we have selected for analysis. The results are rather interesting, but to a large extent alarming. The most alarming discovery is that among the eighty-seven contributors to the sample books on international aid and the conditions in Africa we have chosen, there is only one technologist and not a single agriculturist! The rest belong to various categories of little practical value to Africa: politicians, economists, ecologists, anthropologists, and other academic professions.

The publications we studied fall into four categories: (1) International, (2) British, (3) German, and (4) Scandinavian, and we have chosen one from each group with the following results:

International:

Publication:	*North-South: A Programme for Survival*, Pan Books, London & Sydney, 1980		
Contributors:	18	Economists:	4
Politicians:	13	Journalists:	1

British:

Publication:	*The Study of Africa*, University Paperbacks, London, 1965		
Contributors:	39	Sociologists:	10
Politicians:	11	Journalists:	2
Economists:	4	Various:	12

German:

Publication:	*Afrika und Bonn*, Rohwohlt, Reinbek/ Hamburg, 1978		
Contributors:	7	Sociologists:	2
Politicians:	2	Journalists:	1
Economists:	1	Historians:	1

Scandinavian:

Publication:	*En ny Økonomisk Verdensordning?*, Norsk Utenrikspolitisk Institutt, Oslo, 1980		
Contributors:	23	Journalists:	1
Politicians:	9	Technologists:	1
Economists:	8	Various:	2
Sociologists:	2		

Of considerable interest is that out of a total of eighty-seven contributors, fifty-one (58.6 percent) are employed by universities or research institutes. The total breakdown further shows that there are thirty-five politicians (40.2 percent), seventeen economists (19.5 percent), fourteen sociologists (16.1 percent), five journalists (5.7 percent), and one technologist (1.2 percent). (Note: The group "politicians" comprises active politicians and political scientists. "Economists" include practical economists and academic and research personnel in economic sciences. By "sociologists," we mean persons working or doing research in sociology and in related fields like social anthropology. For the purpose of our study, a further subdivision would serve no practical purpose.) The qualifications of those who consider themselves experts on international aid and Africa, and their fields of expertise are indeed remarkable.

What Africa does not need is politicians, economists, and sociologists. The politicians can talk for the rest of the century, and the economists and the sociologists can do research and write books for years to come, but whatever they say and whatever they find out will be of little importance for Africa. Still, this group comprises more than three-quarters of the experts on international aid and Africa!

Whatever the politicians, the economists, and the sociologists recommend, the Africans will ignore, continuing their own political and social systems without taking advice from Europe or America. In any case, why should they listen to them? Why should Africans listen to politicians, economists, and sociologists who cannot solve their own problems in their own countries? What can they learn from a world where there is a constant economic depression, increasing inflation, and millions out of work? However, in the field of technology and agriculture, in which we are so successful, the Africans know we can teach them almost everything, but among all the eminent people, the prominent people, the important people, and all those self-appointed experts on Africa, there are very few representatives from the fields in which Africans really need help.

Also of great detriment to the way the international bureaucracy tackles the problems of development is the fact that out of our sampling of eighty-seven experts, fifty-two are employed by universities and research institutes. Here again, this is not the type of people who can help Africa. Among the fifty-two, there are obviously many excellent scientists and researchers, but what do they really know of Africa's practical problems? How many of them have worked in the field? How many really know the Africans? And how many seriously think that their theoretical and very academic studies can be of any value for the development of a modern Africa?

Some of them have spent some time in Africa, but mainly as visiting scientists at universities and research establishments there. We have met them all over Africa, as they continue with their learned but futile discussions, in these instances with African colleagues, at the universities in Nairobi, Dar es Salaam, Makarere, Lusaka, Cairo, and Maputo. In the field, out in the bush, in the plantations, or in the factories, they are never to be seen. They have only substituted one academic environment with another.

The saddest part of this story is that so few people are aware that those who are paid by the international bureaucracy and national institutions to aid in the development of Africa are the wrong people doing the wrong job in the wrong organization. As long as the politicians, economists, sociologists, and academic researchers are given the responsibility for planning and carrying out aid, there is little hope for a practical, realistic approach to the problems.

Unable to help their own countries to get out of the economic and political mess in Europe and America, there is even less chance that they can save Africa. It is therefore vital that a new kind of people be employed by the international and national aid organizations. The only ones who can help Africa are the technologists and the agriculturists, but in the international and national bureaucracy they are not even given a chance to prove what they can do in planning aid for Africa.

The superbureaucrats are obsessed with the desire of becoming the world's "leaders," so clearly revealed by their own terminology. They always refer to themselves as *eminent* persons, *prominent* politicians, *high-ranking* individuals, world *leaders*, and *heads* of government. All their activities also receive the same complimentary adjectives, such as *high-level* talks, *high-level* monitoring body, *high-level* advisory body, and *summit* of world *leaders*.

The superbureaucrats, in addition to considering themselves quite extraordinary, have another disturbing feature in common: they are appointed to top positions within the international bureaucracy without having the required professional qualifications for the specific post. They usually are recruited from the ranks of politicians, civil servants, or "prominent" persons in their own countries, which is no guarantee whatsoever that they are qualified even for their national jobs.

Whether it is within Western democracies, Soviet-style

dictatorships, or African autocracies, the world is becoming painfully aware that in modern political life there are quite different qualifications than breeding, education, professional skill, record of achievement, and professional experience that are the prerequisites for important positions within political parties, local and national administration, governmental departments, and the governments themselves. Irrespective of their political systems, politicians are the only group of people who occupy important positions for which they are not trained and for which they normally have no education. While in all modern societies an engineer, a doctor, and a farmer must have the appropriate training, political leaders are doing jobs for which they have no professional qualifications whatsoever.

The whole of the United Nations and all the international committees and organizations are staffed with these people, simply because the top positions are chosen after recommendations from the national politicians and bureaucrats, who never recommend anybody different from their own kind. That is why socialist politicians like Willy Brandt of Germany, Olaf Palme of Sweden, and Third World politicians like Amir H. Jamal of Tanzania and Layachi Yaker of Algeria, can come together and, without the slightest hesitation or trace of modesty, announce for the whole world that they have written a report with the impressive title "A Program for Survival" as a solution to all the problems of the developing countries of the world.

Record of achievement on a national level in the fields in which they are appointed superbureaucrats is no precondition for obtaining the top positions within international organizations. That is why the United Nations Environmental Program (UNEP), with headquarters in Kenya, can have an executive director, Dr. Mostafa Tolba, from Egypt, a country that has solved none of its environmental problems. That is why the United Nations Center for Human Settlement (HABITAT), also in Kenya, can have an executive director, Dr. Arcot Ramachandran, an Indian, from a country where the conditions for human settlement are among the worst in the world. That is why the United Nations Educational, Scientific and Cultural Organization (UNESCO) has as its head a Senegalese politician, formerly minister of education, Amadou-Mahtar M'Bow, from a country with little experience in education and no record of scientific achievements.

What has Egypt done to solve the nightmare of environmental conditions in Cairo and elsewhere in the country that justifies the appointment of one of their nationals as head of the United Nations Environment Program? What experience has India in improving the terrible settlement conditions in places like Calcutta, Bombay, Madras, and elsewhere in the country that justifies the appointment of one of their nationals as head of the United Nations Center for Human Settlement? What has Senegal accomplished in the field of education and science that justifies the appointment of one of their citizens as head of the world's most important international organization in education and science?

Although the top executives of UNEP, HABITAT, and UNESCO are excellent professionals in their own fields, they represent countries with the worst possible records of human environment, human settlement, education, and science and therefore have little to offer the international community from the experience gained in their own countries.

It is one of the tragedies of the international bureaucracy that the top executives, the real superbureaucrats, are not selected on professional grounds. If the U.S.S.R. and the U.S.A. agree about a senior position, including that of the secretary-general of the United Nations, an appointment can be made provided the person in question is absolutely neutral and never has shown any hostility to either of the big powers or the systems they represent. The superbureaucrats are therefore becoming the most impersonal, faceless, and uninspiring automatons the world has ever known. They are men without opinions, except the official ones from UN headquarters. They are men without inspiration, because an inspired idea may be detrimental to their own position. They are men from whom we can expect nothing new, since any deviation from accepted policies is not allowed. The superbureaucrats will state only what we already know. They will write only what has been heard many times before. They will propose only what has already been accepted, and they will discuss only problems for which an official UN answer has already been formulated.

They are men the Africans are supposed to look to for a solution to their problems, but slowly the African intellectuals, journalists, writers, and some of their politicians are coming to the inevitable conclusion that the superbureaucrats are just as sterile and just as useless as the international organizations they represent. They can talk but do nothing else.

The Utopians

Nowhere within organized human activities have there ever been such possibilities and opportunities for proposing the most fantastic, ambitious, and grandiose schemes and projects as within the UN and the international bureaucracy.

Most of their numerous programs and so-called action plans, of which there are literally thousands, are unrealistic from the start. Because there is never any real control over the success or failure of their numerous projects, there is no real danger in proposing and even accepting the most unrealistic program or project. In fact, their only parameter for the numerous organizations, working groups, committees, and subcommittees is the number of programs and action plans that are recorded in the minutes of their frequent and numerous meetings.

This type of uncontrolled and unrealistic activity has

encouraged the appearance of a type of person who now seems to be in senior positions everywhere: the genuine utopian, who will propose anything as long as the magnitude and audacity of his plans and proposals impresses somebody. In fact, it is doubtful if any person other than a flamboyant utopian would survive in a senior position within the international bureaucracy. Anyone who could limit his activities to what is reasonable and realistic would never be noticed. If he wrote reports only about the possible and gave speeches that were down to earth, he would be looked upon as a man without any imagination and devoid of ideas. If one wants to last within the international bureaucracy and be a candidate for a senior position, one has to outdo all the others in grandiose thinking. Failing this, one had better look for another job where realism is a condition for success.

The harm the utopians of the international bureaucracy do in Africa is very serious indeed. The Africans to a large extent believe what the whites tell them. After all, the Europeans and the Americans have built almost everything the modern Africans are in contact with, such as the new skyscrapers in their capitals, cars and buses, transport systems, radio and television, modern airports, and the planes that fly to every part of the world.

Likewise, the whites have sent somebody to the moon, so why should the Africans not believe them when they are told that the deserts will bloom, that they will soon have piped water, housing for everyone, and, before long, enough food to eat?

The Africans are solemnly told that "the UN Center for Human Settlement plans to mobilize resources and coordinate efforts, in and outside the United Nations, to provide adequate shelter and services for these people [the world's poor] and to work for a more equitable distribution of resources as embodied in the New International Economic Order" (Interview with Arcot Ramachandran, executive director of HABITAT, *Kenya Record*, May–June 1979). Does he really think the Africans will believe him? And if they do, how is HABITAT going to fulfill its promises about a utopia where everybody has adequate shelter and services?

The executive director of United Nations Development Program in Nairobi can offer even more to the Africans, assuming they fulfill certain conditions about "a new development strategy to take full account of the environmental degradation that human mismanagement can bring about." If we accept the "new development strategy" (no African is told exactly what that is), there should be few problems. "All men will then have a place in the sun. They will have the opportunity to grow and develop in their own chosen way. They will have congenial surroundings, clear water, good food, shelter, and other good things that environmental resources make possible, and they will have the opportunity to develop and apply the talents of learning, culture, and the arts" (A message from UNEP on World Environment Day, Nairobi *Daily Nation*, June 5, 1978).

An impressive list indeed. Even better than HABITAT's, which promised only better shelter and services. UNEP pledges practically everything, and when it runs out of specific promises, it simply adds "other good things that environment resources make possible" to be certain everything is included in utopia.

When the Africans in Kenya see the impressive headquarters of UNEP outside Nairobi, admire the beautiful gardens, and observe the numerous brand-new cars with red UN license plates that uniformed watchmen let in and out of the closely guarded compound, they must be impressed. They must be even more impressed when they hear all the promises concocted inside the huge UNEP headquarters.

This is the perfect playground for the best-paid utopians in the world. The important question, however, is how long the UN organizations will be able to deceive the millions of Africans who look up to the international bureaucracy as a very competent organization.

Promises come easily to the utopians of any UN organization, and the more unrealistic the promise, the more bombastic the statement. The UN's most important organization dealing with food and nutrition, the World Food Council (WFC), offered in a preamble to the fifth session of the WFC "to facilitate the marshalling of international assistance for those countries with specific food and nutrition plans who are seeking assistance to put them into effect" (*Development Forum*, August 1978). If this is translated from the ambiguous and pompous UN language, it means in simple terms that if anyone has problems with feeding himself or if any country is short of food, the WFC will help! The WFC has rotating representatives —whatever that means—from thirty-six countries, at ministerial or plenipotentiary level—nothing less—who issue the most incredible and unrealistic statements, one after another. Does it never occur to the WFC that to the millions who starve in Africa the action plans conceived by the important bureaucrats on ministerial or plenipotentiary level are pure wishful thinking, a utopian plan that remains utopian because *nobody* knows how to overcome the problems of hunger in Africa?

For the utopian, the spreading deserts that threaten a large part of Africa with total disaster can easily be stopped, and all over the world, newspapers have carried headlines about the plans "to cage the Sahara by building a ring of greenery around it."

At the UN Conference on Desertification (UNCOD), which met in Kenya in 1977, one was told in militaristic terms of the plan for the Sahara "green cage," taking the form "of two international projects, one attacking the desert's northern frontier, the other hitting its southern line of advance." How the desert is to be attacked and hit no one is told, but a feasibility study recommends that "the green belt should be conceived as a wall of trees grown perpendicular to the main wind direction in order to reduce its velocity."

To surround the Sahara with a green belt and to stop the advance of the deserts in the Sahel countries by planting trees might be an interesting topic at UN meetings, but is of no importance to the millions of people in the arid zones of Africa.

As the water holes dry up, the trees die, and the vegetation withers away around the nomads and the pastoral people of the Sahel countries, the various UN organizations try to outdo one another in promoting unrealistic plans and projects. To conceive grandiose schemes can, however, be infectious, and many African politicians are learning fast. Politicians in Nairobi, Dar es Salaam, Kampala, Lusaka, and many of the other capitals in Africa now give speeches about human settlement, food, deserts, green belts, and environment while they adopt the language of the United Nations and the impressive terminology that in reality means nothing. Take, for example, Mrs. Pamela Mboya's statement when she handed over her credentials as a permanent representative to the United Nations Center for Human Settlement: "HABITAT is charged with the task of assisting in the improvement of the quality of human settlements and life in general through technical cooperation and sponsorship of programs to alleviate human suffering and improve human conditions all over the world."

Nothing less than "improving life in general and human conditions all over the world"!

So far, the record for utopian dreams embodied in ambitious but completely unrealistic aid programs is held by Olaf Palme, former Swedish prime minister, well-known social democrat, coauthor of a report on a survival program for the Third World, and an extremely active aid fanatic.

At a meeting in Oslo on October 19, 1980, he managed to propose that the 20 million unemployed in Europe should go back to work to produce goods for the Third World, to the benefit of both the developing countries and industrialized Europe! This was a serious proposal by one of the most active and best-known politicians in Scandinavia. It was not a joke, it was not said as a parody on international aid, and he was not misunderstood. His proposal must represent the limit—we hope—to what socialist politicians in northern Europe can think up as a utopian method for transferring wealth from the industrialized countries in Europe to the Third World. He is not speaking of some natural resources, which we should give away generously. His notion concerns the hard work and toil of hundreds of millions of taxpayers, whom he asks to provide the hard cash for salaries so that 20 million unemployed European laborers can produce goods free of charge to the world's backward and underdeveloped countries. Palme's proposal is not only utopian, not only absurd, but completely insane!

The leaders of the UN and the international bureaucracy will probably remain utopians forever, and nothing will bring them back into a world of realities. The reason for this is simple: if they were realistic, and at the same time honest—which they are not—they would have to declare at every conference they took part in and in every report they published that, with the present system for development and with the present organizations in charge in Africa, the problems of housing, food, water, environment, unemployment, and the advance of the desert cannot be solved. They would have to state categorically that in the developing world, and especially in Africa, people will continue to freeze, starve, live in slums, and be without work, and there is nothing they can do about it.

After living in an imaginary world for so many years and after having obtained the highest positions within the UN and the international bureaucracy by promising more than anyone else, they simply cannot afford to throw away their Fata Morgana of some utopian world they have conceived in their minds. If they did, they would be without the best-paid and most secure jobs in the world.

One day, however, it will be too late to retreat. They may continue with their absurd action plans within their own ranks and within their own organizations. They do, nevertheless, underestimate how long they can fool the Africans.

The intellectual Africans have already seen through the many impressive plans and projects as totally unrealistic. Whenever we have met African intellectuals at universities, research institutes, and government offices all over Africa, we have found that they look upon the activities of the UN and the international bureaucracy as a fraud engineered to deceive the Africans. It is doubtful if the masses of the African people will have confidence in the international bureaucracy for much longer. Maybe the West can send someone to walk on the moon, but its witchcraft does not provide food and water for everyone in Africa or any of the other things promised with such bravado for so many years.

The time for not telling the truth may soon be over, and the last invasion of Africa, an invasion that promised so much but accomplished so little, may come to a sticky end.

4 / The Aid Syndrome

From Friendly Aid to Confrontation

The concept of international aid is entirely new. It is new because the sharp division of the world into developed and underdeveloped countries is new. And international aid is based on the simple philosophy that the developed and wealthy nations should help the underdeveloped and poor nations.

To suit the schematic thinking of politicians, those who later become the aid fanatics, a country must either give aid or receive assistance. There is nothing in between, and the world has consequently been divided into two groups, depending upon a nation's capacity to give, or its need to receive, international aid.

It is difficult to assess what started it all. We have always had humanitarian aid organizations—there has always been some sort of organized help when disaster struck, and there have always been national organizations to look after one's own poor or handicapped. But organized international aid to assist in the *development* of other countries is entirely novel.

After the Second World War, the United States launched

its Marshall Plan, but this was an emergency plan to rebuild war-shattered Europe after a great disaster. This type of help has always been limited in time and to a specific place, and is basically different from the new concept of international aid, which is neither limited in time nor directed to a place where disaster may have struck. International aid is now a concept, not an emergency measure. International aid has become a permanent institution and an omnipresent phenomenon, like national taxes and custom duties, and has acquired a magnitude that is unlike anything the world has ever known before.

It may have all started as token aid from the previous colonial powers. When the European countries left or were forced to leave their colonies in Africa, there was sometimes—but not always—a feeling that the newly independent countries in Africa should be aided during their transition period from colonies to independent states. In the beginning, the new African countries accepted the aid with gratitude, even with surprise, from their previous masters. It was not long, however, before they realized that they could in fact *ask* for more help, which they usually received. What in the beginning was a polite request for assistance, soon developed into *demands* for more and more aid, until the demands were followed by threats.

Between 1950 and 1960, there was a slight increase in international aid, but the change came after 1960 when the labor governments in northern Europe suddenly realized that international aid could be exploited as an instrument for spreading their philosophy of one-world and international socialism.

The influence of countries like Norway, Sweden, Denmark, and Holland on the creation of the present concept of international aid is far in excess of their importance in world trade and international politics. This is due largely to the misconception that the small but wealthy countries in northern Europe could not possibly have political motives for their promotion of international aid, unlike the earlier colonial powers, who were interested in some sort of continued influence over Africa and other parts of the world.

Nothing could be further from the truth, for no country or constellation of countries has used international aid so extensively to promote its political philosophies as have the small but influential countries in northern Europe. These countries are not only giving more aid than any other; they spend proportionately more money on propaganda and information about international aid than all the other countries in the West. And they press with more vigor not only for embracing the present concept of international aid but also for raising the already astronomical financial contributions.

After the early, purely humanitarian aid to newly independent countries in Africa and elsewhere had evolved into a politically motivated world movement, the politicians and the aid fanatics have constantly engaged in all sorts of propaganda for an increase in aid to a larger number of countries.

This has been accompanied by the creation of a new philosophy of aid that is reflected in the use of entirely new terms, definitions, and even a new language, which now can be understood only by the United Nations and its bureaucracy. Every move, every publication, every meeting, every activity of the aid fanatics is in one way or the other politically motivated and is contaminated with political philosophy, and the use of the newly created terminology and phraseology is a reflection of the same.

The term "underdeveloped," coined early in the history of international aid, was later replaced by "developing," while the industrialized world was referred to as "developed." In spite of the fact that the underdeveloped countries are not characterized by development, they are now called the "developing" countries, while the part of the world that is rapidly developing is termed "developed," as if no further development is taking place.

For a long time the world was also divided into the West and the East, and other countries that did not belong to either became the Third World. The West is supposed to be the countries of free democracies like the U.S., England, France, Germany, the Scandinavian countries, and others. The East is not composed of the countries of the east but of the U.S.S.R. and the Communist bloc in Europe. The Third World is sometimes referred to as the nonaligned countries and at other times as the developing countries, tags that have nothing in common.

As if this were not enough, the term "North-South" is now used to add to the confusion. All these terms have no foundation in reality. To group all these very heterogeneous countries into certain constellations with catchy names is simplistic. As P. T. Bauer and B. S. Yamey of the London School of Economics point out: "The idea of a world one-third rich (the North) and two-thirds hungry (the South) is pure fiction" ("East-West/North-South," *Commentary* 3, September 1980).

Underscoring the nature of the concepts, terminology, and language used by the international bureaucracy, Bauer and Yamey go on to state:

Heterogeneous as they are, the components making up the South do indeed share one common characteristic. This, however, is not hunger, poverty, stagnation, exploitation, or colour: it is official foreign aid. The South is in practice the collection of countries whose governments, with a few exceptions, demand and receive official transfers from the West.

Official foreign aid has been the unifying characteristic of this huge, variegated, and utterly diverse collectivity ever since its components began to be lumped together from the late 1940's onward as, successively, the "underdeveloped world," the "less developed world," the "non-aligned world," the "developing world," the "Third World," and now, the "South." These expressions never made any sense except as references to a collectivity of past, present, or prospective aid recipients.

Indeed, without foreign aid initiated and organized by the West, there would be no Third World or South. The outstanding result of foreign aid is to have created the South.

The aid syndrome has now been developed into one of the most complex activities of the twentieth century. It is so vast and involved that nobody can fully grasp the extent of its activities or even hope to control the function of the huge administrative apparatus—the largest the world has ever known—and the numerous bureaucrats it employs around the world. Once a gesture of friendliness, international aid is now but a tool for propaganda and for blackmail, by which one part of the world will forever extract resources and capital from the rest.

The Final Blackmail

The aid fanatics of the West and the greedy countries of the Third World have come together to formulate yet another concept, that of the new international economic order, by which millions of people in the industrialized West will forever work in order to transfer huge sums of money, large amounts of goods, and other forms of resources without any form of compensation or repayment to the developing countries. If the West does not comply, a series of retaliatory measures have been worked out, ranging from cutting off exports of raw materials, to restricting imports or seeking aid and comfort in the Communist bloc. This is the final blackmail against the West, and it is carried out with enthusiastic support by the very people who would be the victims of the blackmail of the Third World: the social democrats of Europe, socialist organizations of any shade and conviction, trade unions, and aid fanatics of all kinds in Europe and America.

During a plenary meeting of the United Nations in May 1974, a special session of the General Assembly convened "to study for the first time the problems of raw materials and development," which resulted in a declaration on the establishment of A New International Economic Order (NIEO). On that day a campaign was launched that would have a most far-reaching effect on the industrialized world and the underdeveloped countries in Africa and elsewhere in the world.

Exactly what the NIEO is was not clearly definable from the first announcement in 1974, nor is it clearly definable today. Like anything else originating from the United Nations and its international bureaucracy, the declaration was shrouded in the most nebulous, inaccurate, and confused terminology, which one hears at international meetings and conferences. What was clear from the beginning —and it has become even more pronounced with the passing of time—is that the NIEO has drawn together all radicals, be they Communists in the U.S.S.R., Euro-Communists, socialists of the West, Social Democrats of northern Europe, or radical intellectuals in Europe, America, and Asia. They have in common one all-consuming obsession: to transfer the wealth of the rich industrialized countries to the poor underdeveloped countries and to establish one form of international socialism under the slogan of a new economic and social order.

For the last six years the amount of propaganda for implementing the NIEO has been overwhelming. Supported by the immense finances of the UN and its international bureaucracy, the world is repeatedly told there is only one solution: the New International Economic Order. Every organization of the UN, such as UNCTAD, UNCSTD, UNIDO, UNDP, UNESCO, and the Center for Economic and Social Information of the UN, takes part in the propaganda. Other branches of the international bureaucracy, such as the Commonwealth Secretariat and the Policy Planning and Program Review Department of the World Bank and international labor organizations, are equally active. Even when unrelated subjects are being considered, as when Apartheid was discussed at a UN meeting in

Nairobi or nuclear disarmament was debated in Oslo, the NIEO is brought into the picture. The strongest supporters of the NIEO in the Third World are those from countries with the poorest records of development in economy, agriculture, and technology. Those who demand most are those who have accomplished the least.

Behind the numerous publications that not only ask for but *demand* that the NIEO be urgently established, one finds names like A. M. M'Bow (UNESCO), Zalmai Haquani (UNCTAD), Bhaskar P. Menon (UN, New York), Shridath S. Ramphael (Commonwealth Experts' Group), and Mahbub ul Haq (World Bank). It is typical that a list like this one comprises people from countries that have not solved their own economic problems, but they want us to believe that they are able to solve the whole world's economic problems through the NIEO. The well-known expert on international aid Professor Gunnar Myrdal is quite correct when in a 1980 interview on Norwegian television he categorically stated: "There can be no successful New *International* Economic Order before the developing countries have established a *national* Economic Order which works."

It is extremely difficult to understand what the NIEO program is. This is partly due to the fact that there is no *definite* NIEO and partly due to the ambiguous language of the UN. The original declaration of May 1974 is full of generalities on colonial domination, foreign occupation, racial discrimination, apartheid, and neocolonialism. It is nevertheless possible to come to a conclusion about some of the main features of the NIEO after all the propaganda, slogans, and general banalities are sifted away. The rudiments of what later developed as the *fundamentals* of the NIEO, were, however, there:

- "Regulation and supervision of the activities of transnational corporations are required."
- "Favorable conditions for the transfer of financial resources to developing countries must be secured."

- "The developing countries must have access to the achievements of modern science and technology."

From this relatively modest beginning, which in reality represented nothing new, the principles of NIEO have been exploited by anyone who wants to transfer huge amounts of international aid from the industrial world to the developing countries without any form of compensation or payment.

In UN terminology, *resources* means hard cash. The real meaning of the word "resources" is a country's collective means of support, but since not even the most greedy ones within the UN have yet developed a scheme for the transfer of the genuine resources of the industrialized world, transfer of resources for the time being means the transfer of huge amounts of capital without any compensation.

The developing countries are not satisfied with voluntary gifts or loans, but demand and insist that this transfer should be compulsory and automatic. This is in reality not new. As early as 1975, Mahbub ul Haq of the World Bank proposed during a lecture on the NIEO at Georgetown, Guyana: "The most important principle underlying a new framework must be a clear recognition by the international community that the resource transfer from the rich to the poor nations cannot continue to remain as totally voluntary acts of periodic generosity: an element of automaticity must be built into such resource transfer."

To support the demand for an ever increasing international aid, a new concept, termed the "redistribution of resources," is slowly being introduced. Even the most ardent adherent of international aid and even the most demanding developing country may find difficulties in persisting in their demands for an ever increasing aid. There are neither moral nor practical reasons for continuing the transfer of huge sums of money forever. Thus we are told, by the UN and by aid fanatics all over the world, that the world's resources are not evenly distributed and that a *redistribution* is consequently justified. For example, in the

UNESCO publication *Moving towards Change* (1976) it is stressed that "the basis and purpose of the demand for a new international economic order is a re-distribution of resources and power." This of course implies—and that is the purpose of this neat trick of propaganda—that the rich industrialized countries have taken resources from somewhere else that do not rightly belong to them. Therefore it is only fair to *re*distribute them.

This completely ignores the fact that countries with large national resources, like the U.S., Germany, France, England, and the Scandinavian countries, are in possession of their resources due to hard work, intelligent planning, and a sound political and economic system. There is therefore no justification for the transfer of resources to countries where hard work is unknown, where all the planning is in chaos, and where the political and economic systems prevent development, as is true of most countries in Africa.

At every meeting of the United Nations Conference on Trade and Development, from UNCTAD I in Geneva (1964) to UNCTAD V in Manila (1979), the problems of prices and markets for commodities and raw materials have been discussed. Like all UN conferences, the UNCTAD meetings produce tons of written papers—during the UNCTAD V, over sixty resolutions were proposed. The main work of the UNCTAD meetings consists of a permanent quarrel regarding programs like the Integrated Program for Commodities (IPC) and the so-called common funds. The demands from UNCTAD and other developing countries for a controlled international economy and a restriction on large international companies are so unrealistic that practically no progress has been recorded at the various UNCTAD meetings. The interests of the industrialized countries, the developing world, the International Monetary Fund (IMF), and the World Bank seem to be in conflict with one another, and most resolutions at the

UNCTAD meetings are compromises—and meaningless, too, for nobody has the competence or authority to carry them out.

The developing countries, the fanatics among the international bureaucracy, and the socialist politicians, who dream about a world where the rich will forever work for the poor, have a common goal they will not deviate from: they are united in a massive onslaught on the world's free-enterprise system. Backed by the largest apparatus for propaganda the world has ever known, their efforts are directed toward "the struggle for a new economic order which should be conceived as a movement which would span several decades and several generations. We are merely at the threshold of this struggle. Our role is that of torch-bearers: to illuminate the ground for those who must follow" (Mahbub ul Haq, "The Third World and the International Economic Order," Ministry of Foreign Affairs, Guyana, 1975).

Equally clearly has one of President Nyerere's advisers, J. F. Rweyemamu, expressed himself: "No longer can the destiny of the world be decided for long by an antiquated power structure [meaning the Western world]. It is with this optimism that we will continue to participate actively in the struggle for the New International Economic Order" (*Africa Guide*, Africa Guide Company, London, 1978).

We are forever to transfer enormous amounts of capital, food, and industrial products, and even to close down our own industries, to maintain a world on a standard of living they cannot provide by their own efforts. Without the slightest regard for the fact that the developing countries in Africa cannot efficiently utilize the enormous resources the UN and its organizations want to transfer from the West, the NIEO has its enthusiastic supporters all over the world.

What is most ironic in the struggle for a NIEO is that the huge international organizations, UNCTAD, UNESCO, UNCSTD, UNDP, HABITAT, UNEP, and many others working for the dismantling of the Western system of economy and democracy, are actually paid for and maintained by the very same industrialized countries they are trying to destroy. Without the enormous financial contribution from the Western world, there would be no organizations to fight the only known system that can grow enough food and manufacture enough products not only to keep themselves in comfort but also to feed and clothe large parts of the rest of the world.

Because of the ever increasing demands and incessant requests for more aid under the New International Economic Order, the Third World is entering into a confrontation with the Western world that it has no chance of winning. By both demanding more aid and insisting that the industrialized countries change their economic and political systems, the advocates of the New International Economic Order will eventually provoke the Western world either to abolish the present form of aid or to develop new forms for cooperation. The NIEO is a threat to the Western world, but in the long run, the Third World cannot profit by threats or provocation.

The Ultimate Folly

Anyone who believes that international aid is a temporary measure meant to help the underdeveloped world during a transition period will be rudely awakened by a 1980 report from the so-called Independent Commission on International Development Issues.

The dreams and visions of the genuine aid fanatics—the real internationalists among leading socialist politicians of Europe and some of the most aggressive representatives of the Third World—have been clearly articulated in the commission's 300-page report on international development issues (later published as *North-South: A Programme for Survival*, Pan Books, London, 1980). What so many people have feared about the ultimate function of international aid has also been clearly spelled out. International aid, according to the report, is meant to be not an emergency operation but a permanent institution and an everlasting system. If accepted, that premise will dismantle and destroy the free-enterprise system of the Western world. Millions of people in the industrialized world—laborers, farmers, technicians, engineers, and scientists—would have to work at least until the end of this century to provide the astronomical tax monies required to pay for a continuous transfer of huge amounts of capital and resources to the Third World.

It all started on September 28, 1977, when Willy Brandt announced at a press conference in New York that he would launch and chair the Independent Commission on International Development Issues, and that the commission's first task would be "to study the grave global issues arising from the economic and social disparities of the world community and to suggest ways of promoting adequate solutions to problems involved in development and in attacking absolute poverty." This commission, often referred to as the Willy Brandt Commission, had eighteen members from a number of different countries. According to the publishers, the commission agreed "with striking unanimity to put forward a set of bold recommendations which would save the world, and if accepted, would indeed amount to a programme for survival."

Throughout the report the commission reveals an obsession for using huge sums of money as the only solution to development problems. Its recommendations reflect the rigid dogma many of its members have inherited from the political movements they represent: that national problems, and now, indeed, international problems, are solved by taking money from the rich and giving it to the poor. The commission grossly overestimates the importance of finance and money. They repeat the mistakes the United Nations's various organizations have been guilty of during the last two decades by accepting the theory that the development of the poor and backward countries in Africa and elsewhere is a sort of automatic process in which the rate of the development depends only upon finance and the amount of available cash. They adhere to the dogma that development is a sort of dormant biological process ready to spring into full life when the limiting factor is removed, and the only limiting factor they seem to understand and accept is the supply of money. In fact, the most important of all resources is not money but the quality of the people involved and their power of accomplishment. Nor are they concerned with *why* so many of the world's nations are backward and underdeveloped. How can anyone who seriously wants to abolish poverty neglect to study the causes for poverty and backwardness? How can anyone cure a malady of any sort without studying the phenomena that are the cause of the symptoms? This is exactly what the commission attempted to do. It diagnosed the symptoms, which it rightly believes will lead to international disaster, but offered no cure, only suggestions for symptomatic relief!

To understand how the backward and poor countries in Africa can be led on the road to rapid development and a reasonable amount of wealth, one must also understand why *some* countries are more developed and wealthier than others.

Some of the most advanced countries of the north, like Germany, Switzerland, Sweden, and Norway, are not wealthy because nature has endowed them with resources that are freely available or easy to utilize. On the contrary, they have developed into some of the most advanced in the world in spite of great odds against them. This was accomplished only through hard work, intelligent planning, efficient administration, and under the protection of a political system that *promotes* development. How can one expect a rapid development in Africa when the existing political and economic systems are characterized by inefficiency, chaos, incompetence, corruption, instability, power struggles, upheavals, revolutions, and suppression of millions of people? The commission ignored the human factor and its importance in transferring modern technology and agriculture to peoples and nations that still have to prove that they also possess the power of accomplishment that made the North what it is today.

The commission's recipe for success is simply to boost all the activities of the present international aid organizations without looking back to analyze what success or failure this sort of aid has accomplished. The commission recommends that the north provide *more* money, *more* funds, *more* finance, and *more* support and that the already cumbersome and ineffective international bureaucracy must be expanded by *more* meetings, *more* conferences, *more* committees, and *more* organizations.

For all the world's problems the commission has specific recommendations. In its report, the commission states that "the elimination of hunger is the most basic of human needs. Therefore we attach great importance to the increase of international food production and to the promotion of agriculture in many parts of the world which have become precariously dependent on imports." It points out that about 700–800 million are poor and destitute, and that 40 percent of them are barely surviving. Although the exact number cannot be known, 500–600 million people are undernourished. But the commission does not ask the obvious question: Why do countries in Africa that have received substantial international aid and have climatic conditions excellently suited for agriculture every year produce less food in relation to their population? Why must the U.S. and other industrialized countries in the West feed several countries in Africa where previously enough food was produced for both home consumption and export? Instead, the commission calculated the millions that must be spent on agriculture and the millions of tons of food that must be provided and stored, suggesting that there should be a food program aimed at "regular supplies of food" and a "system for long-term international food security." Its recommendations state the obvious as a sort of universal truth—"there must be an end to mass hunger and malnutrition." We all know that, but where are the "bold recommendations" regarding increasing food production and eliminating hunger that the publisher of the report so bombastically refers to? There are none. The commission has no other solution to hunger in Africa than the provision of more money and emergency food supplies.

The report does mention that research would have "a large and well-demonstrated impact on production" of food, and that certain agrarian reforms should be carried out "to divide large parcels of land among those who can farm it more intensively." Both statements are based on fallacies. It is not research that is the limiting factor in African agriculture, but the ability of the African to utilize the results of scientific research. And the subdivision of land has never led to high production, of which Kenya and Mozambique are good examples.

One of the most dangerous and misleading statements in the commission's report is "that many countries will take one or more decades before they can satisfy their internal food requirements, and enough food must be made available to them while they are building up their domestic capacity." There is nothing in Africa to indicate that the domestic capacity for food production is being built up, and as the commission itself pointed out, food production often does not increase at a rate sufficient to keep pace with the growth of population.

The commission underlines the danger of overpopulation, pointing out that *one million people are added to the population of the world every five days*, and that nine-tenths of this increase takes place in the Third World. What the commission completely fails to analyze is the effect of international aid programs on the birth rate and population explosion. The dramatic increase in Africa's population is due mainly to all the improvements caused by international aid in the form of food, medicines, and health services.

International aid is therefore to a large extent responsible for the increase in the African population, which in turn demands more aid, resulting in a further population explosion—a vicious circle that has no end but mass starvation.

The alarming effect of providing more food and medicines and improving water supplies is the rapid growth of the African population, which seems not to concern the commission at all. Instead, their only solution is to remedy the situation by information about family planning and birth control. The commission tries to give the impression that family planning works in general, and states that "those who have pursued such programs vigorously, have registered considerable success." In Africa this is simply not true! Take, for example, one of the most advanced countries in Africa, Kenya, where family planning has had no effect whatsoever. But those who read the report may think that the growth of the population is under control. In fact, the increase of the population in Africa is at such an alarming rate that it nullifies all international aid over the last decades.

The commission is also aware that technology is as important as agriculture for the development of the South, and states: "The acquisition of technology is crucial, not only to growth, but for the capacity to grow." The report did not, however, discuss to what extent countries in Africa and elsewhere have the qualified people who can understand, utilize, and exploit modern technology. The commission's only solution is to demand that more technology be transferred to the poor and backward countries.

Regarding the transfer of technology to countries in Africa and elsewhere, the commission has not a single useful proposal or suggestion and instead came with a number of obvious statements that should not take a large, international committee to spend several years to find out. For example, "there should also be greater support for technical assistance, including United Nations Development Programme and its participating agencies," "there should be increased efforts in both rich and poor countries to develop appropriate technology," and "last but not least, there should be more effective co-ordination in the many areas of technology which affect countries all over the world."

The commission also insists upon "broader sharing of technology" and that "it is essential, in the first place, that information about technology should flow more freely, both between and within nations." What does the commission really mean? Technical information is freely available in scientific, technical, and patent literature, and technical know-how is also available if one is willing to pay for it. Does the commission think that technical know-how, which has cost years of research and millions of dollars to acquire, should be given free to the African countries?

The sums that are mentioned throughout the commission's report are staggering. Without the slightest indication of a bold new approach, a deviation in the present aid program, or a new, inspired attitude to the development of countries in Africa and elsewhere, the commission accepts only the constantly increasing demands of the developing world: *more aid and more money*. To add up all the new demands the commission repeats in several places in the report is a futile exercise, but the following statement of the commission is characteristic of its philosophy: "There must be a substantial increase in the transfer of resources to developing countries in order to finance projects and programmes to alleviate poverty and to expand food production especially in the least developed countries."

Here the commission expresses the fallacious premise on which all aid from the United Nations and national organizations is based: that development of backward and poor countries is commensurable with a transfer of huge sums of money from the industrialized world. The commission never doubts the Africans' ability to use the enormous amount of financial aid. While at the present moment many countries in Africa receive so much financial aid that they do not even know what to do with all the money, the commission notes that "Absorptive capacities [that is, the country's ability to spend more money] have to be increased at the same time as levels of aid."

The financing of the enormous increase in international aid is of little concern to the commission, for this will be done by applying new international taxes and levies on the industrialized world. The commission proposes the introduction of *automatic revenue* transfers through international levies on some of the following: international trade, arms production or export, international travel, and sea-bed mining, which the commission finds "a promising possibility."

International bureaucracy, especially the United Nations and all its organizations, long ago reached such proportions that it is completely uncontrollable, and nobody knows what really goes on in the numerous committees, meetings, conferences, congresses, and commissions all over the world. In New York and Geneva alone there are about 6,000 international meetings each year, and the documents connected with those meetings amount to about one million pages every year.

International organizations have degenerated into institutions where men and women talk, discuss, and argue how to save the world from disaster. When little or nothing is accomplished, new committees and new meetings are called, and additional organizations are established to give the bureaucracy and the rest of the world the impression or illusion that they are still working on the problems.

The Brandt Commission is no exception. Throughout its report, it proposes that the already gigantic international bureaucracy in the field of development work be enlarged by a number of new organizations, meetings, and conferences:

• In the introduction by Willy Brandt, it is suggested that

"a summit conference might substantially advance the efforts of the international community to solve the most urgent problems."

- To solve international energy problems, the commission proposes to establish "a global energy research centre under UN auspices."
- The commission also believes that a new attempt should be made to create an "International Trade Organisation which would encompass the function of both GATT and UNCTAD."
- The commission states that "inter-sectoral co-ordination of assistance and country programming [whatever that means!] can make foreign aid much more effective. A first step might be the probing of UN special funds in a UN Development Authority as recommended by a Group of Experts etc."
- Of major importance in the commission's discussion of "an innovative approach to institutional reforms" is the establishment of a new institution that the commission calls the World Development Fund, which "would offer an opportunity for developing and developed countries to co-operate on a basis of more equal partnership and would make universal membership possible."
- As the commission is convinced that what they refer to as "world leaders" can solve all development problems, a Summit of World Leaders is proposed that would "enable initiatives and concessions to be thrashed out with candour and boldness."
- The commission proposes the creation of ill-defined new organizations, such as "a new facility for major additional multilateral finance to support mineral and energy exploitation" and "a high-level advisory body for regular monitoring of the performance of various multilateral organisations in the field of international development."
- The commission is "attracted by a proposal made in 1968 to the UN committee for a Development Planning for

the creation of a body of 12 members from the developing countries and the industrialized world."

To be quite certain that anyone following up the commission's proposals does not run out of the possibility to
participate in a number of new committees, meetings, and
conferences, the commission suggested five "programmes
for development": Immediate Action Programme; Programme of Priorities; Tasks for the 80s and 90s; an Emergency Programme 1980–85; and a Summit of World Leaders. This is international bureaucracy gone mad, expanding
without any thought for the consequences.

Maintaining the Aid Syndrome

The concept of international aid, the theory of transferring
huge sums of money to the poor and backward countries,
the dogma about development as an automatic process, and
the belief that the industrialized world will pay for the
development of the developing countries, all are being
maintained and promoted by propaganda and indoctrination on a scale the world has never seen before.

To maintain this aid syndrome and to finance the ever
increasing international bureaucracy, the United Nations
and all its organizations skillfully manipulate programs
with millions of dollars, which originate from the taxpayers
in the industrialized world, to support new schemes that
require further enormous funds from the taxpayers.

About this the taxpayers in the industrialized world have
no say and can only watch helplessly as the billions vanish
in Africa and elsewhere. The aid syndrome was invented
by and is maintained by the international bureaucracy,
which is paid for with the same money they extract from
every single country in the industrialized world.

The commission's proposal for an automatic international levy, or tax, is the ultimate objective of a philosophy that
considers it a crime to possess wealth and money. What so

many of the commission's members have practiced on a national level will now be carried out on an international scale. If the commission's proposals are carried out, the world has no chance. The hardworking, industrious, and competent people of the industrialized countries will be forced to support countries with huge sums of money where there is no political freedom, where the rich get richer and the poor become poorer, where corruption drains enormous amounts of wealth from the society, where everything is in disorder, where the administration breaks down, where bureaucracy does not function, and where hard work is looked upon not as a virtue but as a curse.

The commission represents one of the most serious threats to international freedom in finance and development work. If the commission's proposals are accepted, and if the industrialized countries are forced to pay huge sums in international taxes, the development of the poor and backward countries will be in the hands of an incompetent and all-powerful international bureaucracy.

In the end, when it becomes clear to all that the present form of aid to poor and underdeveloped countries does not work, the aid syndrome will nevertheless be maintained by the international bureaucracy for no other purpose than retaining the jobs of tens of thousands of bureaucrats holding positions paid for by international taxes.

The commission's recommendations represent a sort of self-perpetuating system that feeds itself and maintains its own growth. The aid syndrome would therefore stay with us forever. To accept the commission's recommendations *in toto* will be to approve the ultimate folly!

Planned Confusion

The most remarkable thing about aid to developing countries is that no one can really define what it is. In spite of the fact that many thousands of people are directly involved in national and international aid, and that the world spends more money on aid than on any other international form of cooperation, there is very little agreement about the definition of aid and development.

How widely opinions differ became quite clear during a recent series of Swedish TV programs (the last one on February 26, 1981), with the participation of people who were experts on international aid. The Swedish Broadcasting System had done a commendable job in bringing together representatives from the official Swedish aid organization (SIDA), experts who had participated in field work in many parts of the world including Africa, and representatives from several political parties and Swedish industry.

What soon became apparent was that there were as many opinions about aid as there were participants in the three one-hour discussions. Some obviously looked upon aid as a politically motivated crusade in the Third World. Others considered aid to be pure charity or some organized way of assisting people who are poor or starving. The discussion was therefore of considerable interest, and to a large extent reflected the opinions found in other countries.

According to the opinions raised during the three TV programs, aid should consist of the following:
• An expression of solidarity between the backward and politically suppressed people on the one side and the rich industrialized world on the other side,
• Organized assistance to improve specific conditions, such as water supplies, agriculture, and small industries, and
• Charity to be given to those who are really poor or suffer from malnutrition and starvation.

It was indeed remarkable that not a single person discussed the very fundamental issue: What is the final goal for all international aid? Is it just to alleviate suffering, is it to build a new type of agriculture, or is it to change the developing countries into modern industrialized societies? We have often posed similar questions to aid personnel in

Africa, representatives from the various aid organizations in Europe, and members of research institutes and university departments, only to find that there seems to be no uniformity to their answers or conformity in their philosophy—and certainly no accord about the definitions. Indeed, in many cases there were no answers at all except that we *must* help them: it is *our* responsibility!

To risk any question after that or to venture a careful *why* would be met with scorn, and we would at once be written off as heartless, unfeeling, and uncompassionate colonials, racists, or something even worse. After this happened so many times, we learned never to question *why* we give aid and *what* the ultimate target of international aid is.

What are the official explanations of why we give aid and the official definition of what aid really is? The definitions and explanations found in publications from the various UN organizations and the international and national aid organizations are vague, imprecise, or shrouded in sentimentality.

Since all aid organizations in the world are geared for helping development, it is extremely important to define development. Aid and development are the two main concepts, but regarding the meaning of the two words there is complete confusion and no agreement whatsoever, as the following examples will clearly illustrate.

In the authoritative Dag Hammarskjöld Report of 1975, prepared on the occasion of the Seventh Special Session of the UN General Assembly, one can find the following: "Development is a whole; it is an integral, value-loaded, cultural process; it encompasses the natural environment, social relations, education, production, consumption and well-being. The plurality of roads to development answers to the specificity of cultural and natural situations."

If any of our students at Nairobi University had written such nonsensical definitions, they would not have passed their test, but the report from which the above quotation is taken is "a product of a collective effort" from a group of experts with the blessing of the UN and many other organizations.

UNCTAD is one of the most important organizations of the UN, and one would expect that their definition of development would be a clear one. With the full authority of the UN General Assembly, resolution No. 1995 (XIX) states the following: "The principal functions of UNCTAD are: to promote international trade, with a view to accelerating development, particularly trade between countries at different stages of development, between developing countries and between countries with different systems of economic and social organizations; to formulate principles and policies of international trade and development; to make proposals for putting the said principles and policies into effect. . . ."

Nowhere is the term "development" defined, although UNCTAD's main function is to accelerate development. UNCTAD has turned into a center for quarrels and fights, which have gotten progressively worse with every UNCTAD meeting. Naturally, one reason for this situation is that they do not know what they are supposed to talk about and what development really is.

When Julius Nyerere in 1974 *forced* 2.6 million persons to live and work in 5,000 villages in Tanzania with a catastrophic drop in agriculture, was that development? At an UNCTAD meeting it probably would be, since anything done in Africa to promote socialism is looked upon as development irrespective of the results of such operations.

For the same reason, the collective and state farms of Mozambique would be development in the eyes of UNCTAD, in spite of the fact that the new rulers of Mozambique have almost wrecked the earlier colonial form of agriculture.

When South Africa forced millions to live in the newly created *Bantustans*, was that development? At an UNCTAD meeting, Bantustans would automatically be regarded as instruments of suppression, and certainly not as development, for no other reason than that South Africa is ruled by whites.

Would the building of new factories by European or American companies in Kenya and Nigeria be considered to represent development at an UNCTAD meeting? Certainly not, since anything done by international or multinational companies in such capitalist countries as Kenya and Nigeria would be considered a further exploitation of the masses.

When the so-called Group of 77 appears at every UNCTAD meeting as a sort of black Mafia with threats of a confrontation with the industrialized world, do they represent the right trends in development, or are they a bunch of reactionary troublemakers? UNCTAD would accept anything they did as development for no other reason than they are black, anti-West, and to a large extent pro-socialist.

Lack of definition, absence of specific goals, and the use of ambiguous terms can lead only to misunderstanding and to endless quarrels, which have characterized every UNCTAD meeting. Every future meeting will suffer from the same difficulties unless the delegates agree on what they are discussing.

There are, naturally, people within the UN and its organizations who are aware of the shortcomings of the administration, structure, and the use of incomprehensible language and meaningless terms. The UN therefore has created a Group of Experts on the Structure of the United Nations System. Judging from their efforts in the field, there is, however, little hope for improvement. In one of the documents submitted to the group for discussion, one can find the following statement: "The necessary breakthrough implies a redefinition of the tasks to be discharged by UN activities and of the measures to be planned, organized and implemented to achieve them; it requires a central policy planning function for the system, which has to be mobilized for this purpose."

Under the heading—which nobody can really

understand—Negotiation Forum and Preparation Function, readers are told: "The fact that successful negotiations do not depend on mechanisms alone, but rather on the balance of power, does not exclude the necessity of adequate and specialized mechanisms. On the contrary, they are needed all the more."

If any of our students in journalism in Nairobi had written such completely incomprehensible nonsense, they would have to rewrite the whole thing. Within the highest paid bureaucracy in the world, which is supposed to lead us to a better future, the use of language nobody can understand or interpret is the rule, not the exception.

Every day, documents are published, reports compiled, and millions of words written, which clarify nothing but only add to the confusion. On a national level the concept of aid and the definition of development are as unclear as they are among the UN and its international organizations. Added to the confusion regarding the concept and definition of development and aid are the different political motives behind the official aid from various countries.

Normally such motives are denied by countries like England, Germany, and the U.S., but some countries state without reservation that their aid has a political motive. This, at least, makes it possible to approach some sort of definition, although it varies from one country to another.

Olav Stokke, a well-known Norwegian expert on international aid, states in his book *Norwegian Development Aid* (Nordiska Afrikainstitutet, Uppsala, 1975) that "the primary target for aid is to further a development which the Nordic countries have tried to create in their own countries." This, of course, defines Nordic aid as an international crusade for a socialist welfare state identical to that of the Scandinavian countries. This definition will hardly be accepted by other countries in Europe or the U.S. And judging by the Swedish debate on international aid, it will also be unacceptable to a large number of Scandinavians.

One of the most extraordinary aspects of international

development aid, therefore, is that there is no conformity and no agreement, and seldom even a definition of either aid or development. Only a bureaucracy is able to continue to work under such conditions. No private undertaking, organization, or industry could ever function—indeed, be established—without having clear, well-defined fields of operation and specific goals. Such nebulous definitions of daily activities and ultimate goals, which characterize international bureaucracy, are of no practical importance to them, for, as we have stressed many times, they have no parameter for success or failure. On the contrary, it is important for the international bureaucracy, the UN and its organizations, and national aid organizations to retain this lack of definition, imprecise formulations, and ambiguous language. After all, who can control what they do, who can pass any verdict on their activities, and who can evaluate their work if there are no precise definitions for what they are supposed to do?

To reorganize, reformulate, and clearly define activities, functions, and goals would require a close and critical scrutiny of the international bureaucracy, and this is the last thing they want. Confusion is therefore an essential part of the whole system. It suits the international and national bureaucracy. It requires that more people be employed, more committees be established, and more reports be written until the confusion is so widespread and absolute that no one can clear up the mess.

5 / The Failures

The Wrong Models for Development

When the Africans took over after the collapse of the colonial powers, they were forced by the politicians in the West, the United Nations, and the international aid organizations into a development that was alien to their own natural desire and ability to progress from colonial rule to a new independent Africa.

The type of development they undertook was not their own but one imposed from the outside by the last invaders of the continent. From the beginning, it should have been clear that the Africans could not succeed. No one could make a success out of a number of development projects that were completely out-of-phase with one another. No one could make models for development work that were desynchronized from the very beginning.

The natural development of Africa and the many African societies may have taken 20,000 years. Maybe the uninterrupted development had taken a longer time, maybe a shorter one. We cannot be certain about the past, but we do know that the Africans' system worked in harmony with their own ability to progress and in balance with the ecology of the continent. Left to their own after the colonial interlude, the Africans would have succeeded as they had done thousands of years before, but to be forced into a development they in reality neither wanted nor were capable of carrying out could only end in failure. There were warnings from men who knew better. There had been warnings in the past, and there will be warnings in the future, but those who want to change Africa into an image of Europe and America will not listen to any advice.

One of the best and most far-sighted administrators of colonial Africa, Frederick Lugard, expressed a view at the end of the last century that has a validity for all time to come, whether it is applied to Africa or to any other nation or race: "A correct concept for development would be one which would enable the natives to maintain their own social and political forms, refined rather than destroyed by the imperial authorities . . . and a system which would allow the native people to develop according to their own cultures" (James Morris, in *Pax Britannica*, London, 1968).

What Lugard asked for, long before the present aid fanatics and international bureaucrats were born, was never granted to the Africans by the aid fanatics and the new international bureaucracy. When they invaded Africa, they told the Africans to develop according to a model they had invented.

The last invaders are not only ignorant about present-day Africa and oblivious to what took place before they arrived, but they also refuse to learn from the present experts in Africa, like Professor René Dumont, who in many publications and in his book *False Start in Africa* has repeatedly warned about the effect of a wrong model of development.

The total accomplishment from the day international aid was started and from the time the Africans accepted this wrong model of development has, therefore, been one of repeated failures. And all over Africa, whether in free-enterprise Kenya, capital-rich Nigeria, socialist Tanzania, or communist Mozambique, the picture is the same: inefficiency, declining agriculture, less food, frequent starvation, expanding capitals with huge slum areas, corruption, political instability, military conflicts, refugees, and sometimes total chaos.

The situation is so bad and is deteriorating so rapidly that a senior African official of the UN Economic Commission for Africa recently stated: "On the basis of all the economic projections we have seen so far, Africa in the year 2000 will not be in the ditch it is in now. It will be in the bottom of a deep black hole" (OECD *Observer*, January 1981).

We cannot blame the Africans. They were asked to do something that cannot be done. We, however, can try to find out what went wrong, and in the following we have studied the development, or the lack of progress, in three different countries in Africa. We have selected for our analysis three different types of political structures in present-day Africa: Tanzania, as an example of African socialism, Mozambique, as an experiment of Soviet-style socialism, and Nigeria, as a capitalist-type country with huge oil revenues.

Tanzania

There are two reasons for choosing Tanzania as an example of the failure of international aid to Africa. First, Tanzania has received more international aid than any other country in Africa. Second, the Tanzanian economy represents a sort of African socialism that is hailed by socialists all over the world as the only system Africans can follow.

The immense aid to Tanzania illustrates very clearly the political motivation behind the aid fanatics in Europe. The socialist and labor governments of northern Europe see in Tanzania a fulfillment of their desire to build a socialist

Africa, and they desperately do everything to make Nyere-re's experiment a success. That is why countries like Norway, Sweden, Denmark, Holland, and Germany have concentrated so much of their aid on Tanzania and have sent so many experts to help in building up African socialism.

Denmark, in its official annual aid report for 1979, explains why: "Tanzania has received considerably more bilateral aid from Denmark than any other developing country. The reason for this is the clear development-orientated policy of Tanzania." ("Development-orientated," a cliché used by all socialists in Europe, means only one thing: that the development of a country is in a socialist direction.)

The aid to Tanzania is out of proportion to the aid to the rest of the continent. The total sum of money that Tanzania has received since independence in 1961 is incredibly large. The exact sum nobody really knows, but the following examples of the flow of aid into Tanzania are a good illustration of how foreign money is used for aid for only one African country.

- The Norwegian aid to Tanzania in 1979 was about N.Kr. 178 million while Zambia, which is just as poor as Tanzania, received about N.Kr. 44 million.
- The Swedish aid proposed for 1981–82 is S.Kr. 440 million for Tanzania and S.Kr. 150 million for Zambia.
- The Danish contribution to Tanzania was about D.Kr. 209 million in 1979, while Danish aid to Zambia is negligible.
- From 1974 to 1976 Tanzania got per year as combined bilateral and multilateral aid from the U.S. the sum of $244 million.
- The total sum received from DAC (Development Assistance Committee of OECD) countries and multilateral agencies in 1976 was about $316,500,000.
- During 1976–77 Canada gave aid amounting to

$14,780,000, which in 1977–78 was increased to $24,990,000.

- From 1972 to 1977 West Germany gave Tanzania loans and grants amounting to more than DM267 million. In 1977 the total sum from West Germany in loans and grants has increased to more than DM787 million.
- Tanzania received Dutch aid during the whole of the 1970s; and in 1977 received grants for $64,180,000.

In addition to direct aid and grants, Tanzania has received enormous loans from a number of organizations, like the International Development Association (IDA) and the International Finance Corporation (IFC), and countries like England, Canada, Sweden, Denmark, Japan, and China. The debt to foreign countries has reached astronomical proportions, and it is impossible to find out the exact value, but as early as 1975 the debt was calculated to be more than $1,192,500,000. This is of little consequence to Tanzania, for the debt will probably never be paid back. In fact, many countries have no choice but to write off the debt, as Sweden did in June 1978.

The socialist experiment in Tanzania is not only aided by direct financial aid but supported by an unusually large number of expatriate experts. During the 1970s there were as many as 5,000 experts working in Tanzania under various schemes, which cost the taxpayers in other countries almost N.Kr. 1 billion or $200 million per year (based on the minimum estimate of N.Kr. 200,000 per expert per year).

There are various calculations and a number of estimates about the ratio of aid to the total development budget in Tanzania. *New African* (March 1979) estimated that foreign aid amounted to 34 percent of the budget over the long period 1961–72. The annual report of DANIDA (the Danish aid organization) quotes a figure for overseas aid to be 65 percent of the total budget for development during 1978–79.

The official Norwegian organization for foreign aid, NORAD, has estimated that during 1979/80 Tanzania paid for only 31 percent of its new development; the rest came from international aid organizations.

More than any other country in Africa, Tanzania has stressed the importance of being independent of foreign countries in attaining its goal of African socialism, on all levels—villages, collective farms, and state-owned enterprises. It has even gone so far as to issue a much heralded document to that effect (the Arusha Declaration), where one can find the following: "Independence means self-reliance. Independence cannot be real if a nation depends upon gifts and loans from another for its development." Brave words indeed from a nation that is more dependent upon foreign aid in grants, gifts, loans, and manpower than any other country in Africa!

Nowhere is it so clear that foreign aid does not work. Nowhere is it so obvious that foreign aid is in fact detrimental to development. And nowhere is it so clearly demonstrated that an increase in aid (as promoted by so many) does *not* speed up development.

Anyone who has visited Tanzania at intervals will have noticed, without seeing any statistics, that the situation is getting worse every year. The more the aid streams into Tanzania, the less can be bought in the shops, the longer are the queues for food, and the more numerous are the unemployed. Everyone seems to be aware of this except the international aid organizations, the United Nations, and national governments, which every year give more aid to Tanzania. Sometimes, however, the truth slips through to the national aid organizations in Europe, and one can read the following comments in the 1979 annual report of DANIDA:

The growth of Tanzania's main enterprise, agriculture, fell from 5.6% in 1977 to 4.6% in 1978. The growth of industry showed a decrease to 4.4% in 1978 compared with the previous years, while in 1979 the situation is even worse. The result is a further reduction of Tanzania's production capacity.

In 1978 Tanzania had a deficit in the balance of payment of 1.8 billion shillings, while the results of 1979 are expected to be even worse.

SIDA (the Official Swedish aid organization) is also pessimistic about the development in Tanzania and stated in its annual report of 1979–80 that "The economic situation in Tanzania has deteriorated further and the economic crisis is now more serious than at any other time during the country's almost 20 years of independence."

However, its Norwegian counterpart, NORAD, seemed to be influenced more by wishful thinking than by the facts—after all, it has given more money to Tanzania than to any other country in Africa—and it stated in its annual report of 1979 that "The economy of Tanzania, seen as a whole, has shown a positive development."

The statement in the NORAD report about Tanzania, which is used to influence Norwegian politicians to give more aid for the following year, is absolutely wrong. There is no positive development, seen as a whole, of the economy in Tanzania. There is certainly no positive development in Tanzania in relation to the fantastic amounts of foreign aid received every year. On the contrary, Tanzania is the example of how international aid in Africa does not work at all.

The view that Tanzania does not live up to its expectations is also shared by most Africans. A special report in *Africa* (October 1976) stressed that socialism is alien to Africa and that "The planning programme is imposed from the top down. Virtually nothing in the guidelines speaks to the need to unleash the creative initiative of the masses, of the symbiosis between top and bottom, party and masses, leadership and cadre." (This is, of course, also a valid criticism against any country in Africa that is experimenting with socialism, like Mozambique and Angola.)

The best-known writer in East Africa, Hilary Ng'Weno, editor of the *Weekly Review* in Nairobi, has pointed out that the "Tanzanians cannot live by political slogans alone," and one may add in the same spirit that international aid cannot exist by slogans either.

The strongest criticism comes from the president himself —which is to his credit. Julius Nyerere points out in his booklet "The Arusha Declaration, Ten Years After" (*Africa*, No. 70, June 1977) that

- Almost all industrial plants are often running below capacity, often as much as 50 percent below.
- Ten years after the declaration, Tanzania is certainly neither socialist nor self-reliant.
- The results of agriculture, the basis of Tanzania's development, have been disappointing.
- State-owned companies are not making enough profit; factories and workshops are grossly inefficient with declining productivity.
- The fact is that we are still thinking in terms of international standards instead of what we can afford and what we can do ourselves.

Julius Nyerere, who is both charming and very intelligent, has two great obstacles that threaten to nullify all his efforts to improve conditions in Tanzania. First, his Chinese advisers, whom he has relied on for many years, and the labor governments of northern Europe, which have given him more aid than any others, have convinced him that socialism is the only way to a new and better Africa. Second, the inefficiency and corruption of his own government departments and the incompetence of his civil servants have made him a leader without people to carry out his orders, like a general without an army.

Either of these stumbling blocks will make progress very difficult, but the combination of the two makes real development almost impossible. Like so many other political experiments in Africa, Tanzania's African socialism was therefore doomed from the beginning, and there is little to indicate that the huge amounts of international aid have had any positive effect on the total development.

Mozambique

The motivation for aid to Mozambique has been even more political than the attempt to support African socialism in Tanzania. The Nordic countries, under their social-democrat governments, have, in this case too, given more to promote socialism in Africa than any other country.

Other countries with huge aid programs for Africa, like Germany, have avoided any direct assistance to the Marxist government of Samora Machel. The total official development assistance (ODA) from West Germany to Africa from 1950 to 1977 was DM8,301 million. Of this fantastic sum, Tanzania received DM435 million, while Mozambique to a large extent has been ignored.

The current official aid from the Scandinavian countries is as follows:

Norway (1979)	N.Kr. 45 million
Sweden (1978–79)	S.Kr. 115 million
Denmark (1979)	D.Kr. 63 million

All the Scandinavian countries plan to increase their aid to Mozambique in the future. The Swedish program for 1981–82 is S.Kr. 210 million, which is an increase from S.Kr. 180 million in 1980–81.

The most remarkable aspect of the aid from Norway and Sweden to Mozambique has been its year-in, year-out support to the FRELIMO liberation movement, which was, and still is, the most extreme Marxist organization in Africa. The total sum given to those fighting for a Marxist Mozambique is difficult to calculate exactly, for some of the aid is channeled to ill-defined activities such as help to refugees and various forms of humanitarian aid.

After Mozambique became independent in June 1975, the new Marxist government nationalized most of the industry and embarked on establishing collective farms and state-owned agricultural enterprises. Private property in land was abolished, and cooperatives of all kinds were encouraged. The authorities in Mozambique are engaged in the largest African experiment in Soviet-style agriculture and state-owned industry.

The Third FRELIMO Congress of 1977 accepted that the immediate target was to raise the production level to that of 1973–74, when Mozambique still functioned as a colony. The more ambitious plan was to establish a true Marxist economy, which finds its expression in Machel's many speeches: "We reject the stagnation of traditional society in which one produces only for subsistence, and we reject the alienation of capitalist production in which each person's task is limited to tightening the bolts or knowing how the machine works. The alternative is the conscious participation of the workers in the production plans for each factory; and the reorganization of the daily life of the masses in which they assume the active role" (*New African Yearbook*, IC Magazines Ltd., London, 1979).

This is like an echo from any conference in the U.S.S.R. and East Germany, where Machel has learned a lot during his many visits. It is also like a revival of the Stakhanovite movement during the Stalin era, which Machel hopes would be their inspiration for building up a new society in Mozambique.

All the versions of old Soviet-style economy are tried out in Mozambique along with some hopeful variations of their own: state farms, *aldeias communais*, or communal villages, FRELIMO cadres, production councils, cooperatives, national economy plans, nationalization, People's tribunals, and *grupos dinamizadures*, or action committees.

All this attracted the labor governments in Norway, Sweden, and Denmark to such an extent that they chose to make Mozambique one of their main countries for official aid. In Mozambique they could experiment with an economic system and a social structure that they had dreamed about for years. In their own countries, the political opposition parties and the democratic system prevented them from fully carrying out their socialist experiments. In Mozambique, however, there were no such limitations. On the contrary, there they found every encouragement for their dreams about world socialism.

This excited the labor governments of Scandinavia to such an extent that they plunged into a field, tropical agriculture, of which they have no knowledge and no experience. In 1977, the Nordic countries and Mozambique signed an agreement for the Nordic Agriculture Program, comprising twenty-six separate projects. Referred to as MONAP, it is an enterprise unique in international aid.

According to Machel, while the implementation of socialist measures since independence "led to a sharpening of the class struggle at national level, and it became necessary for the working classes to have at their disposal a vanguard party, guided by the scientific ideology of the proletariat" (*Africa Guide*, 1978), the labor governments of Norway, Sweden, and Denmark certainly were doing their best to assist Mozambique toward a Marxist society.

To have chosen tropical agriculture as a symbol of solidarity and a field of aid may, however, be a fatal mistake and a cardinal blunder. In modern Scandinavia, one can find some of the most modern technology in the world, and there are experts in many fields within trade, technology, and science. If, however, there is a field about which they know nothing, it is certainly tropical agriculture, and that is exactly what they want to do in Mozambique! Notwithstanding their inexperience in agriculture in tropical Africa, the Nordic Agriculture Program started with a budget of $50 million for the first period of 1978–80.

Tentative approval has also been given by the Nordic Assistance Board to proceed with planning a second phase of the operation (MONAP II) for the period 1981–83, at a cost of $60 million. This will be spread over a total of twenty-three projects, of which ten are new and the rest are retained from the 1978–80 period. The governments in

Norway, Sweden, and Denmark plan to spend a total of $110 million on improving the production of citrus fruit, vegetables, milk, beef, and seed production and to participate in several other projects.

The main agricultural production in Mozambique is limited to a number of important products, such as rice, cotton, tea, citrus, maize, copra, and nuts. All their plantations were built up by the Portuguese, and most of them fell into disuse after independence or suffered from mismanagement by cooperatives and state farms. In order to save Mozambique from hunger and, if possible, to improve agriculture as an export business, it is important to reorganize all the plantations the Portuguese had established and to create new ones. But how does anyone, including the aid organizations in Scandinavia and the bureaucrats in Maputo, imagine that a group of people from northern Europe with no experience in tropical agriculture can accomplish such a feat? Both those who give the aid and those who receive it must realize it will never work out, and the benefits of the aid will be insignificant in relation to the $110 million that will be spent. So far the MONAP projects are mostly failures, partly because from the beginning they were unrealistic dreams and partly because of the chaotic situation in Mozambique.

Reports from international aid organizations are usually optimistic and full of wishful thinking, but in this case, the semiannual report from MONAP published in September 1979 had no choice but to note the following:

- The agricultural sector in general has been unable to meet the established production target.
- The state livestock farms suffer greatly from a shortage of management capacity.
- Present cow mortality on state farms lies in the range of 8–17 percent (5 percent should be the maximum acceptable).
- Fertility rates at state livestock farms range from 35 to 55 percent (85 percent is attained on private farms).

- Production of milk has declined from 5.5 million liters in 1977 to 4.7 million in 1978.
- The average milk production is at 5.5 liters per cow per day (less than half the reasonable production).
- Production of poultry meat in 1978 was only 88.7 percent of the target.
- Production of eggs in 1978 was 79.4 percent of target.
- Production of pork meat in 1978 was 81 percent of target.
- Only 72 percent of all wheel tractors, 46 percent of all band tractors, 55 percent of all light vehicles, and 67 percent of all heavy vehicles are operational.
- Orders for vehicles placed by MONAP in April 1978 will not be fully effected until well into the 1980s due to inefficient government bureaucracy.
- Due to the lack of effective financial control procedures, it is not possible to make more than approximate estimates of MONAP costs.
- The Food and Agricultural Organization (FAO) failed to submit cost data according to the stipulations of the plan of operation. Information on costs for 1978 were received only in July of 1979.
- The Office of the Coordination has therefore not had the capacity to devote adequate attention to develop proper procedures for procurement, financial control, and administration relating to the program.
- The total Nordic contribution available in 1978 was $15 million, of which only 35 percent was utilized.
- Obtaining funds from the Development Bank (BPD) was bogged down for several months due to red tape.
- Recruitment in Portugal is making no progress and appears permanently bogged down in complicated and slow procedures.
- 55,000 boxes from the citrus fruit projects have been lost in the export port of Beira.
- The drainage project at Beira continues to suffer from unfortunate recruitments by FAO, and the lack of cooperation with the local authorities.

The list of complaints and records of poor performance is much longer, but what is quoted here is typical of the problems encountered in any aid project in Mozambique.

There will always be difficulties with the central administration in Maputo, which is extremely inefficient and slow. There will always be problems with the transport of goods and material to Maputo and Beira, where chaotic conditions slow down the imports from overseas. Even the customs authorities cause delays in clearing material that is paid for and supplied by overseas aid organizations. To carry out any project is more difficult in Mozambique than anywhere else and often proves impossible because of the inefficiency and the political philosophy of the authorities.

When the labor governments of Norway, Sweden, and Denmark continue to pour in millions to help Mozambique, they are in fact supporting an attempt to build up a Marxist economy in Africa. Unlike Tanzania, where Nyerere is trying to build a so-called African socialism, Mozambique under Machel adheres to all the dogma of the Soviet-style socialism. Even the propaganda is the same, as the following example shows: "FRELIMO defines its supreme objective as the construction in Mozambique of a society completely free from the exploitation of man by man, where the material living conditions of the people are constantly improving and where their social needs are increasingly satisfied" (*Africa Guide*, 1978).

This has been said a thousand times before in countries Machel looks up to as models for a new Mozambique, countries like the U.S.S.R., East Germany, Poland, and Cuba. For more than thirty-five years the Communist countries in Europe have reiterated that the material living conditions of the people will constantly be improved, and as long as Mozambique survives as a socialist state, it will promise the same. As long as Maputo is covered with red banners and slogans repeating what is found on red banners in Moscow, East Berlin, Warsaw, and Havana, Mozambique will have all the hallmarks and stamp of Soviet

Communism: poor harvests, food queues, shortages, political suppression, secret police, atheism, and suppression of the right to choose.

The total failure of aid to Mozambique is a failure not of the Africans' ability to cope but of a socialist system and a philosophy that is not their own. Aid from the industrialized countries in the West is, therefore, a support for a political and economic system that has worked nowhere else. What never succeeded in Poland, Czechoslovakia, Hungary, and other East-European countries will never work in Mozambique. A continuation of international aid to Mozambique will do little or nothing to improve the conditions. It will instead prolong the agony of a people who have suffered so much already.

Nigeria

Nigeria is an interesting country from many points of view. Independent since 1960, it is the richest, most populous, and most powerful country in Africa. It is also a country in which the rich are unbelievably rich and the poor are incredibly poor.

While the availability of capital in all other African countries, except South Africa, is a limiting factor for growth, Nigeria has sufficient financial resources from oil revenues to make it independent of overseas countries and any form of international aid. Due to Nigeria's strong financial position, its development in Nigeria is therefore followed closely not only in financial circles but by anyone interested in the development of Africa. It is typical that leading journals on Africa, like *New African*, *African Development*, *African Business*, and *Africa*, have at intervals since 1976 published several comprehensive Nigeria surveys. Several research institutes, like the German Africa Institute in Hamburg, regularly publish articles on Nigeria, and in most research meetings and seminars on Africa, Nigeria is an important subject.

In Nigeria it is possible to study what huge amounts of available cash can do to an African country, and what we learn should be a lesson for those who believe that any country in Africa can be developed as long as they supply enough financial assistance.

Nigeria's oil production is around 2.1 million barrels per day and has on occasions reached 2.5 million. Most of the oil is exported to the U.S., and Nigeria's trade surplus with the U.S. alone was $6.5 billion in 1978, rising to almost $12 billion in 1979. Government revenues from oil have been as high as $22 billion, which account for 80 percent of the total revenues. (Statistics in Nigeria, as in all of Africa, are unreliable, and other sources have given oil revenues of only $4 billion per year.) The gross domestic production, which is mainly oil, is incredibly high for an African country, around $50 billion annually.

The population consists of about 200 ethnic groups, with almost the same number of languages. The exact figure of its population is not known, but the estimates vary from 68 million to 80 million. The population figure for the capital, Lagos, of one million is outdated, and some believe almost six million people live in and around the capital.

What is the look of a nation so blessed with huge amounts of the world's most attractive commodity, oil? What is the look of a country that has literally been *given* more money than any other country in Africa? What has been accomplished in a nation where capital is so plentiful that it often does not know what to do with all the hard cash? To find out, one has to go and look at the country, the part of the British Empire Frederick Lugard once wanted to make as a model of an African country.

To visit Nigeria for the first time is quite an experience, and even on the plane from London one can sense the atmosphere of big business. While the rest of Africa turns to Europe and the U.S. for aid, loans, and capital, the situation in Nigeria is the opposite. Those smartly dressed Europeans and Americans traveling to Nigeria do not come with promises of aid; they come to get rich themselves. If ever there was a dance around the golden calf, it would be performed by the business people swarming into Lagos on every international flight. They are eager, full of anticipation, and prepared to do any dirty deal to get the fattest contracts.

When the plane lands near Lagos at the new and very expensive Murtala Muhammed Airport, the first impression is one of extravagance and expensive taste. The second impression is one of aggressiveness and arrogance so different from the conditions one may have been used to in other parts of Africa. The African in Kenya, irrespective of how poor he is, is a gentleman at heart, always smiling and always helpful. Not so the Nigerian. Maybe the wealth of the petrodollars has gone to his head, or maybe he likes to show his overseas visitors that now it is an African who has the upper hand. He will slam the passport down on the table, expect some bribe to get the visa approved or a permit stamped in the passport.

To get through the ordeal at the airport is only the first obstacle. The second one, unlike anything else on earth, is the traffic from the airport to the hotel. There are so many cars among the newly rich, the racketeers, and the foreign businessmen in Lagos that cars are divided into two groups according to the last digit on the license plates. Those with odd numbers are allowed into town every second day, while those with even numbers may be used on the alternate days. Even with this system, which should reduce the cars on the road by half, the whole of Lagos is a permanent traffic jam. The rich African, naturally, has at least two cars so he can drive into town every day, and the poor African can always buy two sets of license plates—at a price. So, cars, from chauffeur-driven Cadillacs to beat-up Japanese imports, continue to clog the city. It is said that the life of the average Lagos commuter is divided into three equal shifts: eight hours at work, eight hours at home, and eight hours in traffic jams.

The driving is wilder than in Teheran, and it is noisier than in Cairo, which no one would think possible. The result is the highest rate of accidents in the world, and the dangers of primitive Africa during colonial time are nothing compared with the deadly risk of driving through Lagos at any time, day or night.

To find a place to live is almost impossible, and at the Eko Holiday Inn, Federal Palace, or some similar expensive hotel, a reservation is no guarantee there is a room available. But for a token gift of a few naira, the same room that was reserved and confirmed suddenly becomes obtainable.

Lagos is a city of contrasts. A few enjoy luxurious houses, expensive cars, and imported food, and millions have no home, no employment, and practically no income. On Lagos Island, skyscrapers compete with slum buildings, and on the mainland, industrial complexes and housing estates are like small islands in a sea of humanity in the most crowded shantytowns found anywhere in the world. What one finds at Lagos is repeated, on a smaller scale, in all the other crowded cities, like Kano and Kaduna. Within a radius of fifty kilometers around Kano, there are at least two million people crowded into modern slums and ancient mud huts.

Kaduna started as a peaceful colonial capital and was carefully planned many years ago by the British military governor Frederick Lugard, a British imperialist who, like another imperialist before him, Emperor Hadrian, was obsessed with planning and building wherever he served his empire. Like Lagos, Kaduna is overcrowded, congested with traffic, and dirty. Those not living in the city itself are found in clusters of mud compounds and shantytowns along the main road leading into the town.

The richest country in Africa is also the worst with respect to poverty, crime, unemployment, and urban congestion. Nigeria has become the Sodom and Gomorrah of Africa, where mammon rules supreme and where the capital, Lagos, has become a monument to capitalism run wild.

While Nigeria in the economic field is unique in Africa, the political life is not much different from that in the rest of the continent. There was never any real democracy after independence, and most of the time Nigeria has been under military rule.

To rule Nigeria, a task not without risks, is often fatal. Prime Minister Tafawe Balewa, General Murtala Muhammed, and Major General Aguiyi Ironsi were all assassinated, while General Yakubu Gowon was deposed. Military rule lasted until Lieutenant General Olusegun Ubasanjo was replaced by the latest president, Shehu Shagari, after the first really free elections after independence. From the political point of view, Nigeria has been neither better nor worse off than the rest of Africa. There have been tribal wars. The worst one was the massacre of the Ibos during the war of independence when the small republic of Biafra was brutally suppressed. Why, then, in spite of being the richest country in Africa, has everything seemed to have gone wrong?

Nigeria's main problem is too much money, not too little. The enormous influx of capital due to oil has not been used to improve the conditions of the majority of the population. As millions get poorer, a few are getting incredibly rich. This has been caused mainly by two factors: agriculture has been allowed to deteriorate in preference to increasing oil production and developing a new, complicated industry; and the curse of Africa —corruption—has been allowed to reach crippling proportions.

Decline in Agriculture

One does not need statistics, FAO investigations, or official government information to see how agriculture has declined in Nigeria. All over the country, small farmers, peasants, and casual farm laborers are migrating to the cities, leaving behind land that used to be cultivated for food and export products. It is estimated that only 56 percent of the population is now rural, which means that 30 to 40 million are living in the towns and cities. (*New Africa Yearbook*, 1979). The decline in agriculture is a catastrophe in itself, but the secondary effect of the rural-to-urban migration is even worse: there are now several million unemployed, and the situation is getting worse all the time.

The oil boom has resulted in too much money in the hands of a few who all the time are investing in new enterprises. Factories are being established with expensive, imported equipment that cannot be used, for there are neither the qualified laborers nor the engineers to operate the machines. New industries are being built for which there is no need in Nigeria. Enterprises that in other countries would be completely uneconomical are established irrespective of cost and availability of labor and materials.

To get into what the investors believe is a profitable market, the most elementary principles of commerce and manufacture are disregarded. The craziest, and under normal conditions completely uneconomical, methods of manufacture are resorted to. For example, to participate in the lucrative market for new automobiles, Peugeot has actually been air-lifting parts for its assembly plant in Kaduna, while Fiat sends the components for its cars across the Sahara to its plant in Nigeria.

Nowhere in the world have elementary principles of a healthy trade and sound engineering been ignored to such an extent as in Nigeria. The reckless and unscrupulous overseas companies are as much to blame as the African entrepreneurs with too much money and no knowledge of industry. There is no real planning, and the many government development plans are only pastime activities of civil servants who have nothing else to do.

Sometimes the results are quite comical. At one stage it

looked like all the world's cement had been sent to Nigeria; freighters were queuing up for months outside Lagos to deliver cement, which soon hardened in the moist tropical climate. There are, naturally, import controls to keep civil servants busy, but the regulations can be circumvented with the necessary bribes, and because everyone who had money wanted to make some more on importing cement, the world could witness one of the most incredible commercial operations ever undertaken.

At least half the industries that are built are uneconomical, but inasmuch as the products can often be sold at incredibly high prices, it will work for some time. Prices for everything are so high that they effectively prevent the millions of poor and unemployed to reap any benefit from the oil boom.

To rent a small house in Lagos usually costs $24,000 per year, and one can get a house only if five years' rent is paid in advance. This is of little consequence to the overseas businessmen whose companies pay the bill, and the local Africans who rent such houses are so rich that $24,000 means nothing.

The uncontrolled extraction of money from the oil industry, the establishment of uneconomical industries, and the dance around the golden calf in the capital and other cities have left agriculture in a shambles. How bad the agriculture now really is, nobody knows, and it is difficult to predict the lasting effects of many years of its neglect.

The Africans themselves are fully aware of the situation, and from African sources we have chosen at random the following comments:
- The governor of Kano State made a forecast in 1977 that Nigeria's annual food import bill would reach N730 million in 1980 (*Africa Guide*, 1978).
- Nigeria spends $1 billion on food imports per annum (*Africa* 111, November 1980).
- Nigeria's food shortage in 1990 could represent up to 39

percent of its total food needs (*Africa* 111, November 1980).

- In 1977 Nigeria paid $750 million to buy food from abroad (*Africa* 95, July 1979).
- In seventeen years Nigeria has turned itself from a net food exporter to a billion-addira importer (*African Business*, May 1979).

The most serious aspect of the decrease in agriculture production is the fact that Nigeria has to pay enormous amounts of money for imported food. The real tragedy is that this huge sum could be paid to the millions of unemployed if they had stayed in the countryside and continued with their farming. The oil revenue could be paid to their own people instead of subsidizing farmers in other parts of the world.

Before the oil boom, agricultural cash crops accounted for over 80 percent of Nigeria's exports, and the government depended almost entirely on them for foreign exchange and government revenue. Today the situation is reversed. Oil accounts for over 85 percent of the exports, and food imports rise year by year (*African Business*, May 1979).

Those who developed the economy in Nigeria have shown extreme short-sightedness and an inability to grasp the realities of the rapid changes brought about by the oil boom. Every new government and every new group of civil servants have had only one goal: to acquire personal wealth by any legal or illegal method before the next government threw them out of office.

What takes place in Nigeria, and what has taken place from the time oil revenues started to flow into the country, is precisely formulated by the *New African Yearbook* of 1979: "The elite's ambition was to acquire wealth by any means. Little or no concern was shown for the interests of the poor, and the result was acute social inequalities. Income inequalities continued to increase rapidly. Food prices and rent levels made life virtually impossible for poor salaried officials, let alone the unemployed urban population."

This is a harsh verdict indeed by one of the most authoritative publications about Africa. When the system collapses, the final verdict will be even more severe, and the total balance sheet will be one of complete failure and bankruptcy. Nigeria, which has more wealth than most other countries in the whole world, has failed to bring a new and better life to its millions and has succeeded only in producing an incredibly rich, but useless, elite.

The Role of Corruption

Nowhere has corruption, the real curse of the continent, played such a devastating role as in Nigeria, where corruption has been developed and refined to a system that controls all economic life. In addition to the usual types of bribery and corruption that can be found all over Africa, the Nigerians have developed the special system of *dash*, which is emminently suited to the conditions in the country. A special report in *Africa* (no. 95, July 1979) estimates that about 90 percent of all business in Nigeria done between Western companies and Nigerian institutions is based on *dash*, which is an unofficial payment made by the seller to encourage the buyer to purchase goods.

The sums of money changing hands are often huge. On one multimillion-dollar order for a construction contract for which the competition was particularly fierce, a *dash* of 30 percent is understood to have been paid out. (Normally, the *dash* is between 10 and 15 percent of the purchase price.) Because lots of money is often involved, Nigeria has quite a number of people who have become millionaires overnight. *Dash* encourages government officials to buy equipment that is not needed—Nigeria is full of advanced and expensive equipment that is not used—instead of spending money to improve agriculture or to establish sound, efficient industries.

The possibilities for corruption are without limit, and the Nigerians seem to be able to exploit them all. Not only do the civil servants receive their *dash* directly, but inflated contracts are awarded to Nigerian agents of foreign companies. The extra profit is divided among the civil servants who issue the order and import permits and the agents who purchase the material overseas.

Every politician since independence has promised to put an end to corruption and maladministration. The latest president, who represents the first civilian rule for many years, Shehu Shagari, is no exception. He is just as dishonest and hypocritical as all the others who preceded him, and he has no qualms in lecturing the world on which he blames the miseries in Africa.

In a recent address to the United Nations he stated the following: "In spite of the enormous natural wealth and resources of Africa, our continent remains the least developed and our peoples the most deprived. These degrading disabilities mock our political independence. What was needed was for the UN to launch a Decade of reparation and restitution for Africa, to enable the continent to recover economically. I have seen too much of Africa's misery and degradation not to be moved to action. We must refuse to subsidize the economies of the rich by continuing to sell cheaply our raw materials and labour in return for exorbitantly priced manufactured goods" (*Africa* 111, November 1980).

With the lack of logic typical of many African politicians and with a complete disregard of the actual situation in his own country, President Shagari criticized exactly what the politicians in Nigeria—and he is one of them—have been doing all the time. It is the elite, which Shagari represents, that makes "manufactured goods exhorbitantly expensive" because of the corruption and widespread use of *dash* in Nigeria. It is impossible to sell anything cheaply in Nigeria from overseas because of the quite substantial amount of *dash* demanded by importers, agents, and government officials.

It is so convenient to blame somebody else. Without

using the precise words, President Shagari implied that it is the international companies and the neocolonialists who are responsible, referring to the age-old cliché of buying raw materials cheaply from Africa and in return selling manufactured goods at exorbitant prices.

Wrong Options

Nigeria is a sad example of an African country where too much money, greed, corruption, and incompetence have wrecked all hope of a better future for all. It is doubtful whether Nigeria can ever extricate itself from the mess, which is constantly getting worse.

No colonial power has ever exploited a country in Africa as the African elite is exploiting its own resources, without any thought for the millions of poor or the future of the country.

Africa's experiment in supercapitalism does not work; neither does the attempt to build a socialist economy on the continent. Europe and the U.S. have not offered Africa any option that really functions. On the one side, the aid fanatics and the UN are using Africa as an experiment for a new economic system or a socialist type of economy, as in Tanzania and Mozambique. On the other side, the Western form of capitalism is relentlessly exploiting Africa's richest country without the slightest concern for the consequences. In both cases they find many Africans keen to do the job for them. For example, African politicians and intellectuals in Tanzania and Mozambique are willing to replace their own cultural forebears with Marx, Engels, and Lenin and do not hesitate to force millions of Africans to work on collective farms and state-owned land with little or no compensation. African politicians and businessmen in Nigeria are willing to let the natural resources of their country be exhausted or destroyed and the land to revert to desert or jungle, and they do not hesitate to let millions of Africans migrate to the continent's worst slums as long as they, and they alone, can get rich from oil, which really should belong to the whole population.

Neither system works, and whichever option they have chosen can only end in catastrophe. The fault is that none of the options is Africa's own. They have been forced upon the Africans, and although alien and foreign to Africa, they have been accepted by a few who have the power to rule and decide.

The biggest danger does not lie in the failure of the various political and economic systems as such, but in the refusal of the international politicians and aid fanatics to accept that failure. To deny this only accelerates the trend toward the final catastrophe.

The Europeans and Americans wanted to transform the continent into something that is not Africa. With an unlimited faith in the power of money, they believed that huge amounts of foreign aid and the capital gained from the sale of the continent's own natural resources would in a few years take Africa through stages of development that normally require several generations. They ignored the elementary fact that no one can buy *time*, no matter how much one is willing to pay.

They are trying to compress 100 years into ten, and in the process a whole continent is suffering. Their money has destroyed agriculture, displaced millions of people, created millions of unemployed, uprooted thousands of tribes, destroyed African culture, wrecked social and tribal structures. The greatest failure of international aid to Africa is, therefore, not the thousands of unsuccessful projects and the waste of huge amounts of money, but the detrimental effect it has on disturbing the thousand-year-old equilibrium between man and society and the even older balance between man and nature.

6 / Science
and Technology

The Last Resort

In Africa, the countries are getting poorer in spite of the billions of U.S. and Canadian dollars, German marks, British pounds, Dutch gulden, and Scandinavian kroner pouring into the continent on an ever increasing scale. The aid fanatics and the international bureaucracy therefore have to accept that aid as they dispense it does not work.

During the last few years, the UN and its organizations and all the national and international aid organizations have shown an increasing interest in the use of science and technology in the developing countries. This new interest in science and technology originates from the simple philosophy that what works well in the industrialized world must also work in Africa.

They know, as we all know, that the Western world owes its advanced stage of development to science and technology. In fact, the industrialized countries, with their high standard of living, would never be in the position they are now without their advanced science and technology. To restore some confidence in the future, the politicians, who are the great promoters of international aid, and the international bureaucracy, whose well-paid jobs depend on the maintenance of the myth of successful aid, see in science and technology their last hope for making a success out of the aid syndrome. Inspired by the hope that what worked so well in the industrialized world will also work in Africa, they have embarked on yet another crusade to save the world.

Inasmuch as their philosophy has always been dominated by the extravagant use of money, no matter the field in which they are active, their many new schemes for exporting modern science and technology continues the characteristic transfer of enormous amounts of capital to Africa and the rest of the Third World. Parallel with the increasing interest in transferring science and technology, a broader philosophy and new concepts are being worked out that will fit into a world picture of another type of aid.

Because the type of development aid we have become used to does not work, the concept of the New International Economic Order was created. This is, however, not enough. Today we are told about the New International Order, which is quite different from the New International *Economic* Order, and yet another concept is created that is called simply "Another Development."

The new philosophy behind the creation of these new concepts is just as nebulous as the old ones and shrouded in the usual incomprehensible terminology of the international bureaucracy, as the following examples (*Development Dialogue* 1, 1979) will show:

Another Development is geared to the satisfaction of all human needs in their inextricable mix of material and political components.

The potential of a new, genuine, North-South dialogue is seen as an important factor of confidence in the feasibility of Another Development and a New International Order benefiting the people all over the planet.

Like all the activities of the international bureaucracy, there is nothing modest about their statements. Nothing less than the "satisfaction of all human needs" will do for the international bureaucracy, which at the latest stage of aid euphoria has even started to think in cosmic terms of our *planet* Earth!

The philosophy behind the transfer of science and technology, Another Development, and a New International Order is being accepted as the last resort and the remaining possibility for creating an international aid system that might work. Even another terminology is coming into use with the coining of fashionable expressions like "autonomous capacity" in science and technology, the "struggle for self-reliance" and "indigenous Third World science and technology." That an artificially created terminology like this (no scientist indulges in the use of such language) should be understood by the Third World politicians, who have no background for understanding the real meaning of such terms, is irrelevant. What is important is that it sounds impressive and can be used at all their meetings and in their publications.

Although the use of science and technology in developing countries has been discussed for decades by the international bureaucracy, it was only recently seriously looked upon as a way out of the mess created by international aid during the last few years. As early as 1963 a conference was held by the UN in Geneva to discuss the "benefit of science and technology of the less-developed areas." This was by UN standards a small conference. Later, as the possible use of science and technology slowly was understood by the UN and national and international aid organizations, the whole mighty apparatus of the international bureaucracy directed its efforts to a meeting in Vienna at the end of 1979. The United Nations Conference on Science and Technology for Development (UNCSTD), under their secretary-general, Joao Frank da Costa, put aside all restraints and broke previous records in its demands for a transfer of resources to the developing countries. It also broke previous records in the number of participants and the cost of a conference. According to the UN *Development Forum* (no. 6, 1979) and *New Scientist* (September 6, 1979), the number of delegates was around 2,000, and the total cost of the meeting was about $50 million. While the size of the conference was unlike anything else done before in the field of science and technology and the cost, incredibly high, the proposals and resolutions adopted by the delegates also reached a new peak in a lack of realism.

The conference used several days to establish what we all know. It was stressed that the industrial countries contribute around 95 percent of the world's total expenditure to research and development, and that only about 6 percent of the existing patents are held by the Third World. It was repeated by almost all the delegates ad nauseam that because the industrialized nations did almost all the research and possessed most of the modern technology, they also controlled the power structure of the world. The delegates from the developing countries looked upon the almost total monopoly of the industrialized world in the field of science and technology as an enormous source of power. And the representatives of the developing countries demanded an increasing part in this power structure.

The Report of the Independent Commission on International Development Issues, which most enthusiastically supports every single *demand* from the conference, refers to a proposal at the Vienna meeting that the Third World's part of research and development should be increased from 3 percent in 1979 to 20 percent in the year 2000.

To accomplish this task—and nobody knows whether it is at all possible—it was further proposed that the industrialized world provide $2 billion before 1985 and another $4 billion before 1990 to aid the Third World in developing their science and technology. In addition, the secretary-general of the UN was asked to provide a mere $250 million for 1980–81 before calling another conference together just to talk about future plans for science and technology in the developing countries.

At the conference, there was nobody who could explain why the sums of $2 billion and $4 billion were necessary for reaching their target of transferring science and technology to the developing countries, and there was nobody who could explain how they had precisely come to these enormous sums. Delegates from Africa, Asia, and other parts of the less-developed world several years ago had politely asked for some $100,000, and later insisted upon millions, but now they are demanding billions.

The developing countries found support among the social democrat countries of northern Europe. Representatives from the industrialized West considered the requests absurd, while delegates from the Communist bloc simply ignored the demand for financing such huge sums and insisted that aid of this nature should be on a voluntary basis. The Third World not only asked for a huge transfer of money but demanded that technical know-how and patents should be made available without any compensation, in spite of the fact that technology in the West is to a large extent the property of private firms.

Before the UNCSTD meeting in Vienna, a number of national and international meetings were held in various countries to prepare the delegates for the oral battles that play such an important role at every UN meeting. In December 1978, the Dag Hammarskjöld Foundation, in cooperation with the International Foundation for Development Alternatives, held a five-day seminar in Uppsala, Sweden, to discuss the "development of a Third World autonomous capacity in science and technology."

The theme of the seminar was outlined by the editor of *Development Dialogue* (no. 1, 1979), which is published by the Dag Hammarskjöld Center in Uppsala with support from SIDA. In the usual, unmistakable jargon of the aid fanatics, he states the following:

The main purpose of the seminar was to investigate how Another Development, need-oriented, self-reliant, endogenous, ecologically sound and based on structural transformations, should find expression in science and technology policies, focusing on the need for countries and institutions in the Third World to develop their autonomous scientific and technological capacity in a spirit of collective self-reliance. The aim was also to explore areas of mutual interest between the small industrialized countries in the North and the countries of the Third World. In order to achieve these objectives and to arrive at practical policy suggestions, the participants had been invited on the basis of their activities at the interface between policy-making and research and in the context of their work for a New International Order.

In an important meeting, where many of the issues for the forthcoming UNCSTD meeting in Vienna were discussed, one could with some justification expect that scientists and technologists who had actually worked in Africa and other parts of the Third World would be invited. For a seminar on the autonomous capacity of science and technology in the Third World, this would be a reasonable condition for participation in the meeting. Most of the delegates, however, were from national and international bureaucracies, universities, research organizations, and government departments. The delegates from Norway came from the Institute of Sociology at Oslo University and the International Peace Research Institute in Oslo. There were delegates from the Sorbonne's School for Advanced Studies in the Social Sciences, in Paris; the Committee for Future Orientated Research, in Stockholm; the Center for the Study of Development and Participation, in Lima; and government officers from a number of countries.

The seminar in Uppsala repeated all the clichés of the UN and the international bureaucracy and added a few new ones. As in any other similar meeting, the usual attacks on the Western world were to be heard.

The practices of the West, embedded as they are in the pursuit of short-term profit and focused on the control of the resources of the planet, have resulted in widespread environmental degradation.

The contents of technological exchanges between North and South would have to be modified accordingly, calling for a drastic reappraisal of the present asymmetric relationship and for bold and imaginative experiments with new forms of Science and Technology Cooperation, including a joint effort to bring under control the activities of the transnational companies.

In the summary of conclusions published after the Uppsala seminar (*Development Dialogue*, No. 1, 1979), we can find the same nebulous statements, the similar unrealistic action plans, and the equivalent language that have become the hallmark of all the activities of the aid fanatics and the international bureaucracy.

Action plans are always more impressive than anything else and should reflect, it is hoped, the dynamic and determined character of those who put them together. The Uppsala seminar was no exception and suggested no less than nineteen proposals under the now familiar heading of "action to be taken."

Even the action plans contained attacks on the common enemy, the international companies of the West. One plan called for "the establishment of international rules for controlling the activities of the transnational companies and of the necessary monitoring machinery in the interest of North and South alike."

What they *really* want to do with science and technology in the developing world remains a mystery and is not made any clearer by statements like: "Thus the endogenous science and technology capacity, in contrast to the across-the-border indiscriminate transfer of technologies, will strengthen the Third World capacities to generate, develop, select and use technologies capable of contributing to socially and environmentally sound alternatives for the production and use of goods and services."

If this is the type of muddled thinking and incomprehensible statements the delegates later took with them to Vienna, it is no wonder the UNCSTD meeting accomplished next to nothing in spite of the presence of 2,000 delegates from all over the world.

The Uppsala seminar was not the only meeting where the delegates prepared themselves for the main battle of the UNCSTD meeting in Vienna. There were literally hundreds of meetings all over the world, of which the Pugwash workshop and conferences at Badkal Lake, Haryana, India, in January 1978, at Rabat, Morocco, in April 1978, and at Varna, Bulgaria, in September 1978, are typical examples.

This traveling jet set of professional aid fanatics produced documents and reports that by comparison made the Uppsala seminar sound quite rational and realistic. The final text of all their deliberations was approved by the Pugwash Executive Committee in December 1978 for transmission to the secretary-general of UNCSTD. The committee concluded: "Thus, in the closing years of the Second Development Decade, and on the eve of the 1979 UN Conference on Science and Technology for Development (UNCSTD), a consensus is emerging to the effect that the Less Developed Countries must build up an autonomous capability for problem solving, decision making and implementation in all matters relating to science and technology for development." This means simply that the backward countries must do their own research, but it took the members of the Pugwash organization meetings in India, Africa, and Europe before they could state the obvious.

Strangely enough, the Pugwash meetings on international scientific cooperation for development did not produce the usual action plans, but made up for it by recommending sixty-two different guidelines for governments, funding agencies, scientists, and technologists.

An Endogenous Science and Technology?

Few of those taking part in these discussions and participating in making new action plans, recommendations, and guidelines are scientists and technologists, and even fewer have taken part in the actual development of science and technology in Africa and other parts of the Third World. The results are therefore as expected. The discussions become oral battles among participants of seminars and delegates to conferences who do not know the realities of the Third World. When they talk about science and technology in Africa, the discussion becomes purely theoretical, and the recommendations they propose can be nothing but hypothetical.

When organizations like UNCSTD, the Dag Hammarskjöld Foundation, and the International Foundation for Development Alternatives discuss the transfer of science and technology to the Third World, where are the European and American scientists, engineers, and technologists who have carried out scientific research, built factories, and run industries in countries in Africa or other parts of the developing world? How often is a scientist or an engineer taken from an African laboratory, technical university, or the assembly line in an African industry to join the international jet set so he can attend meetings in Geneva, New York, Uppsala, Rabat, Varna, Manila, Badkal Lake, or some other exotic place the international bureaucracy favors for their expensive meetings? To find such an expert at these meetings, where he is badly needed, is a rare occasion indeed. The ratio between the genuine expert and all those who know nothing about the theme they are discussing is alarmingly low.

One of the many disastrous consequences of letting the nonscientist and the nontechnologist dominate all national and international discussions about science and technology in the developing countries is the perpetuation of a number of fallacies that originated within the walls of conference rooms in Europe and America.

For example, their endless and repetitive discussions about science and technology that is endogenous, indigenous, autonomous, and self-reliant is meaningless. If ever there was anything that is international, created by all and belonging to all, it is science and technology. There is no African science and technology simply because the principles of science and technology are universal. Whether a transistor is made in Johannesburg, Tokyo, or Berlin, it is still a transistor. Whether nylon is spun in England, South Africa, or India, it is still nylon. Whether a polymer is synthetized in Nairobi, Leverkusen, Oslo, or Chicago, it is still a polymer.

Sometimes, styling is mistaken for technology. There is definitely an Italian car and an American counterpart. No one would make the mistake of thinking the two cars come from the same country. But the science and technology behind both are the same, whether the car was made in Torino or Detroit.

Both authors of this book have done scientific research in Africa and Europe for many years, and we naturally know there is no African or European science and technology. What scientists and technologists do in South Africa, Kenya, and Germany is based on the same thing. It was therefore often stressed among our colleagues at Nairobi University that the curriculum, the textbooks, and the exams were the same as in Europe. There is no African chemistry; the chemistry taught at Nairobi University is the same as the chemistry taught at any European or American university.

All these futile and meaningless discussions among aid fanatics and the international bureaucracy about a sort of national science and technology can only confuse the issue of establishing or improving science and technology in developing countries.

Even the themes for discussion and the titles of publications are wrong and misleading—for example, "Struggling for Self-Reliance in Science and Technology" and "Towards Endogenous Science and Technology for Another Development" (*Development Forum* 1, 1979).

If a country became independent of other countries for science and technology or expected these forms of human activities to grow entirely from within (which is the real meaning of self-reliant and endogenous), no advanced science and technology would develop in that country, and what had already been developed would soon die out.

To transfer huge sums of money to the developing countries ($2 billion by 1985, as proposed by the UNCSTD conference) in order to establish some sort of "African" science and technology is clearly impossible. Africa has no capacity for using such huge sums for science and technology. It has neither the scientists nor the technologists to utilize these staggering sums. Instead of getting involved in hypothetical problems, grandiose schemes, and incredibly expensive projects that can never materialize, international aid organizations should make available a much smaller sum of money for the *existing* scientists, technologists, universities, and research laboratories in Africa. Not thousands of millions of dollars in a few years' time, but maybe a couple of million *now*.

There are all over Africa, at the universities of Nairobi, Dar es Salaam, Lusaka, and the other capitals of the continent, hundreds of excellent, first-class African scientists and technologists who are capable of carrying out high-quality research but are unable to do so simply because they lack funding for new laboratory equipment and maintenance of the old. It would be so incredibly simple to call together the scientists from African universities and research laboratories to find out exactly what they want. With support that would amount to a few percent of the cost of the schemes advocated by the UN and its organizations, science and technology in Africa would get the boost it rightly deserves. By utilizing the existing scientific manpower and given funding they need and are able to use *now*, the African scientists and technologists would be able to prove that they also can do what others are doing in Europe and the U.S. Instead of sending 2,000 delegates to the UNCSTD meeting in Vienna, who used about ten days to argue and quarrel about things they hardly comprehend, they should ask the African scientists and technologists to present their views and requests for funding of the existing institutes and laboratories. For the cost of *one* UNCSTD conference, which accomplished nothing, hundreds of institutes and laboratories in Africa could be kept operative for many years to come.

This, of course, would not suit the hundreds of government departments and private organizations that are kept busy for a year before an UNCSTD meeting takes place. It would not suit the thousands of delegates who travel all over the world, stay at expensive hotels, and spend some time in foreign countries with all expenses paid. And finally, it would not suit the secretary-general of UNCSTD and his numerous, well-paid staff members, who would see their importance reduced, job opportunities dwindling, and a further expansion of their activities minimized. Thus the international bureaucracy that is now in power will ensure that the disastrous road to bigger and more expensive conferences is followed, and it will do its very best to continue the type of discussions on science and technology for the developing world that so far has led to nothing.

The Options

It is part of the schizophrenic thinking of our time that so many aid fanatics and scientists of all shades and convictions are so much in favor of self-reliance in science and technology. In principle, they are the great internationalists, but when science and technology span national borders, they do their very best and use every opportunity to attack some of the most international aspects of human activities within science and technology.

An advanced science and technology can be international only with a great amount of interdependence among countries. Still, they want science and technology to be self-reliant and autonomous. Their philosophy is, here, as in so many other cases, politically motivated. The last thing the UN and the aid fanatics want is to accept development that is based on the economic and political systems of the big capitalist powers like the U.S., Canada, England, and Germany. On the other hand, they believe that Africa must be industrialized one way or the other.

Even during the colonial period, advanced technology was introduced to Africa. James Morris, in *Pax Britannica*, underlines the fact that "the British Empire was a developing agency, distributing technical knowledge around the world, and erecting what economists were later to call the infra-structure of industrial progress—roads, railways, ports, post and telegraphs."

As long as the colonial powers ruled Africa, they constantly upgraded and modernized the technology they had built up on the continent. Even today, many years later, the products of what was at that time advanced technology can be seen all over Africa, and in most cases they are still functioning.

After the collapse of the colonial rule and until there was some semblance of political stability on the continent, the general technology of Africa, including factories, transport systems, ports, and harbor installations, slowly collapsed due to misuse, lack of maintenance, and shortage of spare parts. The Africans did their very best to keep the wheels turning, but established little new industry or modernized the old. Only when a new type of entrepreneur appeared on the scene did Africa enter a period when up-to-date industry was slowly established, erratically at first, and often against great odds due to revolutions, wars, and general political instability. Sometimes the entrepreneurs' efforts failed, due not to incompetence or lack of capital but to wholesale confiscations in the name of nationalization. In most cases, however, their efforts were crowned with outstanding success where the conditions were favorable, as in Kenya and, for a shorter period, in Tanzania and Zambia.

The new entrepreneurs came from the U.S., Canada, England, Germany, France, Italy, and many other European countries. They had enormous resources in capital and highly skilled men. They had almost unlimited access to research, science, and technology, and shared among themselves almost all the available experience and know-how of building, running, and maintaining modern industries of almost every kind.

The entrepreneurs were the huge international companies that depended upon almost every branch of modern technology, engineering, transport, chemistry, electronics, machinery, instrumentation, mining, forestry, and agriculture. They had one thing in common: wherever they operated, they were always successful unless their efforts were made impossible by political, legal, or military conditions.

The success of the international companies was there for everybody to see. The very nature of their operation made success a necessity. They could not, like the organizations of the UN and international aid, afford failure, and if they failed, which did not happen often, their enterprises were either closed down or completely reorganized. Left to themselves and with the support of sympathetic governments, they could only succeed; and for this very reason the UN and international aid organizations from the very beginning started a campaign against the international companies operating in Africa and elsewhere. The international companies are looked upon as a sort of competition by the UN and the international aid organizations, and every opportunity is used to insist that the international companies be "controlled" or that ethical and moral standards be internationally imposed on their operations.

So great is its animosity toward the international companies that the UN has adopted a special terminology to use against them. First of all, the term "international" is not used any longer. To be international is a virtue, but the newly coined terms "multinational" or "transnational" could, with the backing of enough propaganda, be given an odious meaning. The term that was finally accepted is "transnational," which is clearly being used to indicate that the international companies stood *above* all nations instead of promoting work *among* the nations. And because the word "corporation" suggests capitalism, the term that will stay with us is "transnational corporations"—though in most cases they are neither *trans*national nor corporations.

Especially the social democrats of the countries in northern Europe, representatives of the Third World, and bureaucrats of the UN and its organizations dream about the time when they can restrict and even forbid the operations of the international companies. For the time being, they have to be satisfied with some sort of control as the first attack on international companies. This possibility they are exploiting to the fullest, as the following examples will show:

Regulation of the transfer of technology must obviously be combined with measures to control transnational corporations which are gaining an increasing hold on the economic and trading chances of the developing countries (*UNCTAD for a New Economic Order*, United Nations, New York, 1978).

Underlying many of the fears about multinational corporations, both in the South and the North, is the concern that they have been able to race ahead in global operations out of reach of effective controls by nation-states or international organisations; that they have been able to benefit from economic disorders at a time when many nations have suffered from them . . (*North-South: A Programme for Survival*).

Even UNESCO, which ought to deal with activities other than the world's industry and agriculture, uses every opportunity to attack the international companies, and even goes so far as to recommend a system that would "enable member countries to protect themselves from the harmful effects which may be attendant upon the activities of transnational corporations" (*Moving Towards Change*, UNESCO, Paris, 1976).

The UN takes for granted that the behavior of international companies is immoral and unethical and repeatedly asks for control of these companies. Typical is the opinion of the UN Commission on Transnational Corporations expressed during a meeting in Lima in 1976: "The Commission's most important decision was on the issue of a code of conduct for international companies, to which it clearly assigned the highest priority" (*Global Dialogue*, Center for Economic and Social Information, New York, 1977).

The UN has even established a Center for Transnational Corporations (UNCTNC), which certainly will not recognize their good work but rather monitor and eventually, it hopes, control their activities. The UN even published a very comprehensive report—"Multinational Corporations in World Development" (New York, 1973)—after collecting an impressive amount of data and information to be used against the international companies.

The opinion of the role of international companies is the same in the Communist bloc and in the West—in fact, the former is greatly responsible for creating this opinion now so vigorously raised by the UN and the international bureaucracy. A well-known study by Soviet experts on Africa asserts that "the young African states have in the international corporations a new and very dangerous enemy" and that "the most modernized instrument of present-day neocolonialism in fact is the international corporations" (*Neocolonialism and Africa in the 1970's*, Progress Publishers, Moscow, 1978). Scandinavian publications, of which *Norway and the Third World* (Universitetsforlaget,

Oslo, 1979) is typical, join in the criticism of and the demand for control of international companies.

Judging from all the propaganda against international companies, one would think they represent almost all the evils of the world. In fact, all the operations of international companies are made out to represent another form of colonialism. The international companies are branded as neocolonialist; they are seen as the instruments of the form of Third World exploitation that the industrialized countries had to resort to when the old colonial empires were dismantled.

Occasionally a lone voice can be heard in the wilderness. Take, for example, the statement of the Commonwealth Experts' Group, published by the Commonwealth Secretariat (London, 1976), which was prepared to "recognise that transnational enterprises can have a positive role to play in the industrialization process of the developing countries, because of their command over finance, technology and access to markets and their capacity to plan, establish and manage complex operations."

Even less frequently do the international companies defend themselves against all the attacks or explain why their activities are beneficial to the countries where they operate. The following are statements from two typical international companies, one in the field of agriculture, the other in engineering.

A new business venture is seldom profitable in the early years of development. Certainly that was the case with the pineapple operations that Del Monte began developing in Kenya in 1965. Until production capacity was expanded in 1975, volume was not large enough to result in profitable operations.

Following a $20 million expansion of our operations, Kenya Canners began earning profits upon which it paid required taxes. This business now represents a major new industry that provides an average of 4,500 year-round jobs, an apprentice training program to aid employees in developing job skills, and generates $30 million in foreign exchange that the government of Kenya needs to finance the import of goods that it doesn't produce for itself.

The launching and efficient operation of a major processed foods export business requires a great deal of technical knowledge about agriculture, processing, engineering, and distribution. Del Monte made a sizeable capital investment in Kenya at the request of the government and with the encouragement of the local community. This venture made Kenya Canners a major employer and foreign-exchange earner that provides significant economic benefits to the local area and to the country. (Michael P. Roudnev, Vice President for Public Affairs, Del Monte Corporation, in *World Paper*, September/October 1979.)

I can't speak for all multinationals, not even for all manufacturing ones. But Ford Motor Company's experience with direct investment in developing countries has been extensive. We have manufacturing or assembly operations in 10 developing countries. We have been in some of these for over 50 years, and in most for more than 20. On the whole, our operations in these countries have been successful and satisfactory to both the company and the host governments. Productivity is the key, and that key is most accessible through the multinational corporation. You can look all around. You can study all the learned treatises on development, but you won't find a source of productivity that is more effective on an international scale, or more able to go to work right now.

No matter where you are, it consists of four basic elements: First, it's bringing capital to bear on human needs through machines and facilities; Second, it's bringing the talents of people to work on those same problems, people with brains and technological ability to invent new designs and processes; Third, it's getting somebody to organize and manage the people and the capital and the know-how, and to train other people to help them, so that everyone involved can extend his effort a hundred-fold. And that's particularly relevant to the Third World, where you're almost starting from scratch in many cases, with a completely unskilled labor force. Fourth, and last, it's a climate of investment that every government sets, negatively or positively, through regulation and taxation.

The multinationals provide the best available linkage with the markets, technology and know-how of the industrialized world. Through direct foreign investment in plants and equipment, they also provide a ready source of capital without adding to the debt burdens of the developing countries. Multinationals have been called the most creative economic invention of the 20th century, an "engine of growth" that can accelerate development the world over. But instead of being welcomed and sought after by the developing world, they are, in many cases, being discouraged from seeking investment opportunities there. (Lee A. Iacocca, President of Ford Motor Company, "Multinational Investment and Global Purpose," *Topic* 115, U.S. International Communication Agency.)

The most successful form of international aid to Africa is the activities of the international companies—a fact that cannot be contradicted even by the massive propaganda against them by the UN, international and national aid organizations, and socialist and Communist governments in Europe. They are responsible for creating numerous new positions at all levels, and often employ the educated African in administrative and technical positions. Very often they plow back a large portion of their profits into new ventures or modernization of existing plants and factories. In many cases, the international companies have neither the majority of the shares nor full control of the management. The advantages to the local population in the various African countries are therefore obvious. Without the international companies willing to take the risks of operating under extremely difficult political conditions, there would be a catastrophic decline in the development and establishment of new industries and modern plantations in Africa.

It is therefore so much more deplorable that the UN and its organizations, as well as many national aid organizations, advocate control of the international companies and are actively engaged in a malicious propaganda program that in its extreme form describes the international companies as a new and very dangerous enemy of Africa's young states.

Instead of trying to control the activities of international companies and instead of labeling them as the new colonials of Africa, developing countries should encourage international companies to invest in Africa. Before it is too late, the African countries should heed the warning of the editor of the American magazine *Topic* (issue 115): "It is better to make a multinational feel at home than make them wish they were back home!"

Appropriate Technology

We have discussed how the UN and the various aid organizations on both a national and international level have unwillingly accepted that the massive aid to developing countries does not work satisfactorily and that science and technology for the last few years have been looked upon as the last hope for improving the conditions in the developing world.

The acceptance of science and technology as the last resort for aiding the developing countries has caused an almost schizophrenic attitude among many aid fanatics and international bureaucrats, especially those who look upon international aid as a tool for spreading ideas about international socialism and a new world order. The conflict is caused by the fact that the only real transfer of technology to the Third World has been done by the international companies. In their eyes these huge international enterprises represent the most advanced form of capitalism and a last attempt to regain control over the old colonial possessions in Africa and elsewhere. Because they see no other way of building up a modern, advanced technology in the Third World than through these companies, they are doing their very best to discredit their operations.

Even the most ardent and unrealistic aid fanatic understands that the UN and the rest of the international bureaucracy cannot attempt to transfer technology and build industries in Africa and elsewhere. To accept modern, advanced technology is to acknowledge the superiority of the West. Torn between these conflicting ideas, the UN and the aid fanatics have come up with the ingeniously simple idea of appropriate technology, as distinguished from advanced technology.

"Appropriate technology" is the latest slogan that has brought together politicians, aid fanatics, and international bureaucrats of widely different backgrounds and people holding even opposite political views. For some, appropriate technology is the symbol of the struggle against international capitalism and neocolonialism, for others, appropriate technology is an expression of their hopes for an ecologically sound development of the developing countries. The new concept has united the cynics and the dreamers, who now believe they have the final answer to development problems anywhere in the world.

Appropriate technology is now discussed at every meeting of the UN and the international bureaucracy that deals with development. It is considered an important subject by institutes and research organizations, becomes an important aspect of national and international aid organizations, and is even discussed by the governments, parliaments, and national assemblies in Europe and North America and has become a household word all over the world.

In spite of the widespread and universal acceptance of the new term "appropriate technology," there is no general acceptance of what it really means. Like so many other concepts created by the UN, such as a new international economic order, "appropriate technology" has no accurate definition. As the term now is being used, it is completely meaningless. Practically all technology is appropriate. A rocket engine that takes a lunar module to the moon is certainly appropriate; otherwise it would not get there. So is an electron microscope used to study viruses, for there are no other means to make a virus visible to the human eye. A small handpress to produce a few kilograms of oil from seeds is also appropriate, but it is not the right thing to use if the production target is a few tons.

Some associate appropriate technology with primitive technology, while others think that any simple device represents appropriate technology. This is still no precise definition, since there is no agreement about the terms "primitive" and "simple." An African blacksmith or operator of an old hand loom will get visibly annoyed if his methods are referred to as primitive. At the same time there are very advanced pieces of machinery that are simple. A ram-jet engine is extremely simple compared with a twelve-cylinder aircraft engine, but installed in a missile, it certainly represents an advanced method for locomotion.

In spite of the fact that the term "appropriate technology" is without any clear definition, it now plays an important role in almost all aspects of international aid. (To add to the confusion several other terms are used as synonymous with "appropriate technology," of which the most common are "village technology" and "intermediate technology.") We cannot find an exact definition of "appropriate technology," but it is important to know what the UN and the international bureaucracy *think* it is, and the following statements will give us some idea:

The call for appropriate technology does not prescribe any particular type; much less does it imply that technology should not be the latest or the most sophisticated. It means that the choice of technology should be a conscious one, taken in the knowledge that it can affect the character and direction of development (*North-South: A Programme for Survival*).

The choice of appropriate technologies and the degree of reorientation would vary with the specific factor endowments and development objectives. Appropriate technology must be seen as the mix. No single pattern of technology or technologies could be considered as being appropriate, which contributes most to economic, social and environmental objectives (*Development Forum*, January/February 1979).

Interest is appropriate, i.e. simple, low-cost indigenously-based technology as a means of improving the quality of life for families and their children, stems from the realization that no other form of technology could effectively serve, at affordable cost, the millions of very low income families throughout the rural areas of the developing world (*Village Technology in Eastern Africa*, UNICEF, Nairobi, 1976).

By an appropriate technology we mean a technology which, in the context of development measure, is appropriate to the natural, economic and social conditions prevailing locally. As local economic and social conditioning are dynamic factors, the appropriate technology must also be considered as dynamic (*GATE* [German Appropriate Technology Exchange] 1, May 1980).

It is doubtful if anyone becomes wiser from studying the definitions of appropriate technology in publications from the UN or national and international aid organizations. Inasmuch as there are no precise definitions or guidelines for appropriate technology, the activities of those engaged in promoting appropriate technology become just as confused as the term itself.

One day in Nairobi, we were invited to the Kenyatta Conference Center to witness the demonstration of a piece of appropriate technology that, according to Calestous Juma, of the Environmental Liaison Center in Nairobi, would save Kenya nearly 125,000 tons of charcoal or 1.5 million tons of wood from 313,000 hectares of land. Since one of us was teaching the use of energy at Nairobi University, this was good news, and we both went to the combined meeting-demonstration to see how we could reduce the wood consumption by one and a half million tons per year.

Behind the new invention was a scientist with the Geneva-based Bellerive Foundation for Primary and Renewable Energies who worked in close cooperation with the Environment Liaison Center in Kenya. Backing up the demonstration of the new energy-saving device were the

National Council for Science and Technology (NCST) and the Ministry of Energy in Kenya.

With great expectation and considerable curiosity, we waited for the moment when the new invention would be unveiled. When it finally happened, we did not believe our eyes and doubted we heard correctly. After the minister of energy, Dr. Munyua Waiyaki, had given his speech about the new *jiko* (a small charcoal stove), we were allowed to inspect the new device. There, right in front of us —onlookers, the press, government officials, representatives from research organizations, and dignitaries of all kinds—was a small charcoal burner of a type we had seen by the hundreds many times before. The principles were exactly the same as those utilized by the charcoal-burning stoves made from sheet metal by the Cape Coloureds in South Africa, or the wood-burning stoves made from cast iron by the early pioneers in the American wilderness as they moved West a hundred years ago.

This is a sort of appropriate technology that is completely misleading to the Africans. It serves no purpose except as the playground for overseas organizations and scientists who like to experiment with gadgets of all kinds under the misconception that they create appropriate technology.

With support from the UN and European and American aid organizations, all sorts of appropriate and village technologies are promoted. In Kenya alone there are Village Polytechnic programs that stress the use of appropriate technology in spite of the fact that the African students are eager to learn the most advanced technology. They do not want to learn how to solder together some water cans of galvanized steel or how to preserve heat by putting a cooking pot in a box of hay. To them, appropriate technology is a waste of time. They want to learn a profession and a technical skill they can use for securing a post in a factory or workshop. It is a misconception that the African wants to learn appropriate technology. He wants to do what the white man does in his factory.

Often the teaching of appropriate technology is only confusing to the students. To combine solar heating, which is entirely new to the African, with the making of mud bricks, which is an ancient craft all over Africa, is neither here nor there. This is, however, what is done at the village technology level, and can only add to the muddled thinking of what appropriate technology is and what it is meant for.

As the Africans are introduced to appropriate technology, the international bureaucracy is busy doing their part by establishing organizations and holding meetings to promote appropriate technology all over the developing world. UNICEF is an enthusiastic promoter of appropriate technology, and in 1976 it held a seminar in Nairobi about simple technology for the rural family. In 1978, the United Nations Industrial Development Organization (UNIDO) arranged an international forum on appropriate industrial technology. The forum was held in two parts. First, 314 scientists and other specialists from forty-seven countries met for a week in New Delhi at what was termed a technical/official level. This was immediately followed by a three-day ministerial-level meeting, in the town of Anand in Gujurat, attended by representatives from twenty-nine countries.

Meetings like this do not contribute to the understanding of appropriate technology. Neither do the many other meetings where technology transfer or appropriate technology are discussed, such as the comprehensive conference of the European Association of Development Research and Training Institutes held in Milan during September 1978.

Early in the development of the concept of appropriate technology, organizations were established to deal with this problem, like the Intermediate Technology Development Group, for which Dr. E. F. Schumacher, author of *Small Is Beautiful*, was largely responsible. Another addition to organizations of this nature is the German Appropriate Technology Exchange (GATE), an off-shoot of the main

German development agency, the Deutsche Gesellschaft für Technische Zusammenarbeit (GTZ).

The name of the German organization is somewhat misleading, since there cannot be any *exchange* of appropriate technology between Germany and the Third World. The dissemination of information will be a one-way traffic, and considering German thoroughness, inventiveness, and faith in technology, it is difficult to believe that this information will be as simple as appropriate technology.

The Germans' pride in advanced technology makes it very difficult for them to produce anything that could be considered "appropriate technology." GATE certainly does not get bogged down in making charcoal burners or soldered water cans; it produces equipment for regenerative energy, solar energy, wood gasification, ethanol, wind energy, and biomass, which all require a thorough knowledge of physics, chemistry, and microbiology.

It would be very un-German if they had come up with simpler answers, and German minister of research and technology Dr. Volker Hauff therefore had to give some justification for the use of advanced German technology by stating, "I do not think that modern high technologies and the satisfaction of basic needs necessarily contradict each other" (Interview, GATE 1, May 1980).

The Final Choice

Africa cannot afford to make yet another wrong decision with regard to the models for development. If the Africans had been allowed to develop at their own pace and according to their own abilities, appropriate technology could have worked. In fact it might have been a natural development.

This is, however, about one hundred years too late. A systematic and large-scale transfer of advanced technology may make parts of Africa look like the Ruhr district in Germany, Birmingham in England, Pittsburgh in the U.S., and the Donetz Basin in the U.S.S.R. This may be the last thing Africa wants, but on the other hand, while appropriate technology may be ecologically sound, it will never provide the manufactured products Africa so badly needs. To choose appropriate technology now will never solve the problems of productivity, either in agriculture or in industry. The Africans will therefore no longer have the privilege of making a final choice of their own free will. Nor will they be given the time to experiment.

If the continent is to survive, and if the millions are not to starve to death, they must soon choose a model for development that will keep them alive. The time for making a decision is very short, and the options are very few indeed.

7/ Produce or Perish

The Decline

The harsh reality in Africa is that whatever system was tried for development, it did not produce the desired result. A report by the president of DAC, part of the Organization for Economic Co-operation and Development (OECD) and the article "Focus on Africa" in the OECD *Observer* (January 1981) spell out in clear terms that the productivity of African countries is almost stagnant or even declining and that the growth of their export volumes has slowed down and even gone into reverse during the 1970s.

In sub-Saharan Africa, each person has on the average less access to food than was the case ten years ago, and average dietary standards have fallen below the minimum nutritional requirements. Average food production per person has steadily declined since 1960. Meanwhile, during the 1970s, Africa's annual population growth of 2.7 percent was 14 percent higher than the average for developing countries generally. During the 1980s, when population growth in the rest of the developing world is projected to turn downward, it is expected to rise to 2.9 percent in Africa.

During the 1970s, the growth of per-capita income in the low-income countries of sub-Saharan Africa averaged only 0.2 percent annually, compared with 1.1 percent in the low-income countries of Asia and 2.9 percent in developing countries generally. Per-capita income in low-income Africa is expected to increase by only 0.1 percent annually between 1980 and 1985 and by 1.1 percent between 1986 and 1990. More-conservative estimates predict that the real income in the poorer African countries will *decline* by 0.3 percent annually between 1980 and 1985, to become positive again (0.1 percent) between 1986 and 1990. The facts are now there for everybody to see. After twenty years of independence, after getting rid of what the Africans consider colonial exploitation, and after being given more aid and assistance than any other continent has ever received, the development in Africa has slowed down to such an extent that the catastrophe is there already.

The great tragedy of Africa is that after the African countries have become independent, food production has not increased proportionally with the growth of the population. Africa is today a hungry continent, and it is getting worse every year. How bad the food situation is, nobody knows, but every year the newspapers are flooded with reports of the starving millions. The exact figures for the number of people suffering from malnutrition and actually starving can only be estimated, and the figures quoted by the UN, various aid organizations, and the Red Cross vary considerably.

Starving Africans make good news, and every year the news media are flooded with telegrams, articles, and pictures telling a grim story of hunger in Africa. The following is a random sampling from the press in Africa, Europe, and U.S. dealing with hunger and malnutrition in Africa that underlines how serious the situation really is.

A climatic shift is bringing death and starvation to six countries in West Africa. The lives of nearly 40 million people are threatened by a catastrophe of terrible proportions (Cape Town *Cape Times*, October 6, 1973).

Ten thousand die from starvation in Ethiopia, and the number of dead will probably reach 100,000 (Oslo *Aftenposten*, October 8, 1973).

Some ten million people are weakened by hunger and malnutrition in the six nations of French-speaking West Africa (Pasadena *Plain Truth*, November 1973).

More than 1,000,000 hungry nomads are roaming the Sahel, surrounding its cities in a futile search for food (*Time*, December 17, 1973).

A recent government study in Ethiopia's Shoa province found that 12,000 people had died of starvation (*Time*, April 8, 1974).

In Niger alone, the shortage of foodstuff is expected to be 300,000 tons in 1974 (Pasadena *Plain Truth*, June-July 1974).

A billion people go hungry (Oslo *Aftenposten*, October 25, 1974).

At least 460 million people are threatened with starvation, and ten million will probably die this year (*Newsweek*, November 11, 1974).

There are millions of potential hunger victims across Central Africa, from Somalia and Tanzania to Zaire and Guinea (Johannesburg *To the Point*, April 18, 1975).

Seven million people are suffering from malnutrition in the Sahel countries (Nairobi *Weekly Review*, March 13, 1978).

The number of undernourished people in the world continues to increase. 400 million at the end of the 1960's, and 455 million in the first quarter of the 1970's (UN *Development Forum*, August 1978).

Seven million people are threatened with starvation in the Sahel region of West Africa (Cape Town *Scope*, August 25, 1978).

Sixty million people starving to death (Nairobi *Sunday Nation*, February 11, 1979).

The Third World, in particular Africa, must import increasing amounts of food (Reuters interview with FAO director E. Saouma, in Rome, August 1979).

Tanzania is faced with acute famine and its worst crisis since gaining independence from Britain 19 years ago (Nairobi *Daily Nation*, March 19, 1980).

Over 12 million people may starve to death in the area from Chad to Somalia (Oslo *Aftenposten*, June 7, 1980).

A million and a half tons of food are needed over the next year in East Africa (*Africa*, August 1980).

Starvation faces millions in parched Africa (Johannesburg *Sunday Times*, August 8, 1980).

1,400,000 threatened with starvation in Africa. 30,000 died from hunger in Karamoja in Uganda last year (Associated Press, February 8, 1981).

For more than ten years now, the international community has been watching hunger and famine in Africa, unable to do anything really to help or to abolish hunger on the continent. The UN has naturally held meetings, adopted resolutions, and published articles. The national and international aid organizations have increased their budgets for supplying food and medicine. For many years the UN publications have been full of impressive articles about "a world food security system," "plan for faster food flow," and "the billion-dollar food fund." There have been a multitude of "food conferences" and ambitious programs to save the starving Third World. As early as 1976, the UN and the World Food Council came up with what they referred to as "a three-tiered proposal which would provide a substantial measure of international food security," which consisted of the following:

- A 500,000-ton emergency world reserve to meet unexpected food shortages on the order of those experienced in the Sahel, Ethiopia, and Bangladesh
- The earmarking of national reserves to secure a dependable level of food aid, insulated from market forces
- A security reserve of 15 to 20 million tons to serve as an insurance mechanism and to forestall sharp fluctuations in world food prices

At that time—June 1976—Kurt Waldheim was promoting the establishment of an International Fund for Agricultural Development (IFAD), to be supplied with more than $1 billion from the industrialized West and the OPEC nations (UN *Development Forum*, June 1976). In 1978, the World Food Council suggested at their meeting in Mexico that the UN General Assembly convert the 500,000-ton international emergency reserve to a permanent, annually replenished reserve and at the same time try to persuade various governments to increase the reserve to 10 million tons (UN *Development Forum*, August 1978). Apart from supplying huge stores of food to fight hunger in the Third World, the only other form of assistance the various UN organizations seem to understand is to increase financial aid. According to the Report of the Independent Commission on International Development Issues, the developing countries may need *additional* assistance to agriculture of between $4 billion to $8 billion per year up to 1990. The International Food Policy Research Institute (IFPRI) estimated at the same time that the aid programs in the field of agriculture should be $12 billion annually in the 1980s! (In view of these grandiose schemes, which in a decade would run into hundreds of billions of dollars, it is slightly amusing that among all the projects in the billion-dollar bracket, we can find the following recommendation: "The rich of the world could also help to increase food supplies if they ate less meat." *The Brandt Report, North-South*, Pan Books, London, 1980.)

In addition to all the meetings, all the discussions, and all the impressive proposals for feeding the millions who are hungry, hundreds of publications ranging from small pamphlets to huge treatises, such as the UN study *The Future of the World Economy* (Wassily Leontief, et. al., United Nations, New York, 1977), appear regularly to give their contribution to the problem of the world's hungry.

There must have been thousands of pages written on this subject by the UN staff, economists, and scientists of all kinds, but their contribution to assuring food for the millions is exactly nil. It does not mean a thing to those who starve in Africa that some European or American sits down and writes about the international development strategy and alternative scenarios of development. The African is not interested in academic treatises; he desperately needs food now. In spite of all the food programs, all the money from international aid, and all the impressive research on food and hunger, the situation in Africa is not improving.

But more surprising than the lack of results is the reluctance to accept that the present methods for controlling hunger do not work. The UN and the international bureaucracy will never learn, and instead of accepting defeat, they just plan to continue on the same road that has led nowhere. In a special OECD publication on Africa (*Focus on Africa*, January 1981), under the type of heading so adored by the international bureaucracy, "The Scenario for the Push," the only suggestion offered for improving the conditions in Africa is to get together for just another meeting. That is all OECD can say after twenty years of aid, after billions have been wasted, and after American and European farmers have for years grown food to keep the African alive.

The Wrong Choice

Nobody seems to be interested in *why* African agriculture has declined the way it has, and no one seems to be able to explain what happened to the potentially rich agriculture in Africa that once was described in the following words: "There were maize stalks twice the height of a man [in Kikuyu-land in East Africa], and vines of sweet potatoes, the huge flaglike leaves of arrowroot, various varieties of plantains, tree beans, bunches of bananas, tobacco ten feet high with eighteen inch leaves, sugar-cane grown for beer-making, and cattle, goats and sheep in pastures lying fallow" (*African Rainbow*, H. K. Binks, Sidgwick and Jackson, London, 1959).

How could it then all go wrong? How could a prosperous development be stopped and even reversed? How can the rich soil, and the potentially rich and productive agriculture, decline, and how can the soil of Africa not even feed its own people, let alone feed other countries, as it once upon a time did?

The answer is simple. The Africans made a wrong choice, with catastrophic results. They ignored the experience of the settlers who had farmed successfully in Africa for almost two generations. They neglected the heritage of the past and forgot that the richest gift to the Africans was the fertile soil, which, with Africa's tropical and subtropical climates, could easily feed Africa and many other parts of the world. The African politicians and the African leaders were suddenly devoted to another type of development: the establishment of industries, the erection of factories, and the building of a new infrastructure that would support their new visions about a modern Africa.

They forgot about their agriculture and set about making industrial products, which in reality could be made much cheaper somewhere else. They assembled cars that could be exported to them from the modern robot factories in

Cologne, Wolfsburg, Coventry, Torino, and Billancourt much below the African manufacturing costs. They built steel mills when steel mills all over the world run below capacity and can supply any country in Africa with all the steel wanted and at very competitive prices. They assembled electric and electronic equipment that can be made much cheaper in Europe, the U.S., and the Far East.

The Africans' mistakes were not theirs alone. They were guided and aided toward the wrong models for development by politically motivated aid fanatics, enthusiastic but ignorant international bureaucrats, and the United Nations, which used Africa as a huge laboratory for their costly experiments.

The most serious mistake the Africans made after they gained their independence was to ignore completely what the colonials and the settlers had learned about African agriculture. They listened to all the socialist politicians and intellectuals, especially in England, who told the Africans that the colonial type of agriculture was designed only to exploit the Africans. All over Africa the white settlers were therefore chased away, their farms were bought for very little, and quite a number were simply eliminated.

In some countries, the new black rulers behaved like gentlemen and paid a reasonable sum for the farms, as in Kenya. In others they behaved like thugs, and stole and confiscated everything, as in Zaire, Angola, and Mozambique. Irrespective of what methods they used to take over the agriculture that had been so successfully developed by the white settlers, the results were usually the same. A large number of farms were divided into uneconomic units; others were turned into state farms or collective enterprises. Where they still believed in private undertakings, as in Kenya, a large number of the big farms and plantations were bought up by the newly rich African politicians, who had neither the time nor the knowledge to run the big farms efficiently. For them, it was not a question of returning to the lands of their forefathers; it was a simple way of investing money accumulated from corruption, shady deals, or plain smuggling.

For some peculiar reason, socialists in Europe and radicals in the U.S., like the Africa experts in Moscow, argue that everything the white settlers did with African agriculture was wrong. This has brought catastrophic results for the Africans, who have been unwise enough to accept all the Marxist and radical philosophy.

No one has put this unfounded criticism in such simple words as Susan George (author of the well-known book *How the Other Half Dies*): "Africa is also one of the outstanding victims of another system guaranteed to create and perpetuate hunger: the cash crop. That so many young nations have not yet rid themselves of colonial agricultural patterns inherited from a world they never made, is one of the great tragedies of our time" ("How the Other Half Starves," *Africa*, March 1977).

Because the Africans were made to believe that anything colonial was both evil and nasty, they set about tearing to pieces and wrecking what the colonials and settlers in Africa had needed hundreds of years to establish—a modern, efficient, and scientific agriculture—instead of preserving almost two generations of knowledge and experience and building the new African agriculture on that sound foundation.

One would think that Susan George and all the others who show such hostility toward the white colonials and settlers had never heard about men like Lord Delamere and all the others whom Elspeth Huxley describes in the following way: "When Lord Delamere first entered the Kenyan Highlands in 1897, he was amazed by their grassy downs and cedar-forested slopes and saw in the British East Africa Protectorate a country of great latent wealth waiting only for a plough and ox. Six years after his first visit to Kenya, the young Lord Delamere and his wife took up land in the Rift Valley, determined to show by example that crops and livestock could be made to thrive and to prove to the world that this was a white man's country. In face of pest, illness, costly failures, stock-thieving, labour and political crisis, Delamere struggled with ultimate success to grow crops on land that had never before been cultivated, and to breed livestock on pastures where only Masai tribesmen had intermittently roamed" (*White Man's Country*, Chatto and Windus, London, 1974).

People who blame the agriculture of the colonials and the settlers for the failure of the present-day agriculture in Africa ignore completely that it was this agriculture that made Africa prosper for almost a hundred years. They also forget the simple fact that colonial agriculture *had* to be successful. The British in Kenya, Uganda, Rhodesia, and South Africa; the Portuguese in Mozambique and Angola; the Belgians in the Congo; the Germans in Tanganyika and southwest Africa; and the French in west and central Africa—they had no international aid that poured billions into Africa if their agriculture failed.

The effect European agriculture had on the African population and the extent to which it exploited cheap labor are quite different matters. As agricultural enterprises, they were the most effective and successful Africa ever had. Therefore, the Africans should have preserved, not torn to pieces, what the whites had built up through hard work over many years. There is nothing wrong with the concept of cash crops, which the socialists and radicals see as the very symbol of colonialism. It was the only crop the colonials could sell, it was the only product they could make that brought in profit. This is exactly what Africa needs today: it must produce crops or goods that can be sold in Africa and exported to the rest of the world. There is no other choice.

Africa is again confronted with the problem of whether to divide the land between the poor for subsistence farming or to do farming on a large scale, which produces crops that bring in profit. This is exactly the problem the white settlers were confronted with almost a hundred years ago when they introduced large-scale modern agriculture. The current problems have therefore been solved before, a long time ago, but everybody seems to have forgotten the experience of the past. What was said in 1893 is repeated today with the same justification:

While the soil of Kenya and Uganda, to be sure, was uncommonly fertile, African farming methods, barely adequate to a subsistence economy, were not expected to bring the regions out of the red for at least two decades.

If East Africa were to become self-supporting in a relatively short time, the transformation must be brought about through high-volume, high-quality agricultural production, managed on modern lines and grown on European farms" (Charles Miller, *The Lunatic Express*, Ballentine Books, New York, 1971).

The Only Alternative

It is now an indisputable fact that with the present type of agriculture, Africa cannot feed its growing population, and it grows little to obtain foreign currency for the import of vital raw materials and manufactured goods.

If Africa is not to be dependent on charity, aid, and support of all kinds, it must *grow*, *process*, and *manufacture* enough products for itself and for export. If Africa cannot increase its production of agricultural crops and manufactured goods, there are no possibilities for Africa to extricate itself from the vicious circle of more aid, more loans, and increasing debts. And if Africa cannot in the nearest future increase its capacity for production, it will not have another chance. Africa will starve, and millions will perish.

Whether these products are raw materials or finished goods is immaterial—in one way or the other they have to be produced or manufactured. This capacity to produce and the ability to create something where there was nothing before is the only real parameter for development.

To accomplish this, hard work cannot be substituted by anything else, and there is no substitute for intelligent work. Only this can lead to products the Africans can eat, products they can wear, and products they can sell. The Africans must reject the numerous models for development, which never work in practice, created for them inside the conference rooms of the UN and the international bureaucracy. They must make their own program for survival, not letting the radical left of the Western world prescribe for the Africans what they will do.

If the Africans are willing to learn from the past, to acknowledge the experience of the most successful farmers Africa ever had, the European settlers, and to use the most efficient technology the world has ever seen, that of the American farmers, they will be successful.

This is a question of accepting a few basic principles, of which the following are the most important:

- Africa must produce crops that are specifically suited to the soil and climates of Africa. Only in this way will African agricultural products compete on the world market.
- Africa must produce crops that can *feed* the continent, concentrating on the traditional staple diet of the African. Only in this way will Africa eliminate expensive imports of food.
- Africa must base its industry on those agricultural raw materials that are cheaper and more plentiful in African countries than anywhere else, and it must utilize the experience and knowledge of the international agro-industry. Only in this way will African industrial products be able to compete on the international market.
- A new infrastructure must be developed by the Africans themselves by mobilizing the millions of unemployed to use traditional methods for building roads, water canals, irrigation systems, and storage facilities. This infrastructure must be geared exclusively to the needs of the

mechanized agriculture and advanced agro-industry. Only in this way can Africa become really independent of international aid and loans.

- Africa must accept that a dualism will continue for generations: the development of modern agriculture running parallel with the traditional, tribal economy. Only in this way will the problems of forced and artificial development be avoided.

If their agricultural products are to compete on the international market, Africans have no choice but to use the most modern and efficient methods for tropical and subtropical agriculture. If they want to develop an industry and sell the products on the international market, they have no alternative but to use raw materials that are cheap in Africa or unavailable in other countries. Africans must give up as completely unrealistic the notion that they can manufacture goods that can compete with the products from the latest robot industries in the U.S., England, Germany, France, Italy, and Japan. Any of the industrialized countries of the West can manufacture industrial products and sell them cheaper in Africa than the Africans themselves can make them.

On the other hand, in the field of agriculture, Africa has advantages that no other continent has. But labor-intensive agriculture, which is vigorously advocated by all national and international aid organizations, is a myth and makes an efficient utilization of Africa's natural resources impossible. In fact, the degree of mechanization in agriculture is almost directly proportional to the degree of development and the standard of living in any country. Subsistence farming, or agriculture based on traditional and appropriate technologies, will barely keep African farmers alive, and the only way to improve this is to use methods that will not only support the farmer and his family but will feed a number of other people as well.

Success in agriculture is almost synonomous with overall

success, as the following data (*Time*, November 6, 1978) clearly illustrate:

Country	Number of people fed by one farmer
U.S.	59.0
Western Europe	19.2
Japan	13.7
U.S.S.R.	10.0
World Average	5.1

There is no exact data on African countries, but the figures for them are below the world average. In fact, in most African countries, the average African farmers have no surplus food to sell. The only country in Africa that can feed its own population and export huge quantities to other African and overseas countries is South Africa. And the only reason for this unique situation is that South Africa has practiced for a long time what we have proposed as the only feasible type of agriculture for the rest of Africa.

African agriculture is emminently suited to produce food, sugar, fibers, nuts, and seeds, which are the foundation for modern agro-industry. Practically all the products —maize, sugar cane, cotton, jute, vegetable oils, fats, and a variety of tropical and subtropical fruits and vegetables —can be processed, thereby producing valuable end products that can be sold on both the local and the export market. Fibers from cotton and jute must be turned into textiles and clothing; seeds from plants must be processed into oil, soap, and chemicals; maize, cereals, and nuts must be treated to produce high-protein food, oils, and fats; and other crops that can be grown in enormous quantities, such as sugar cane, must be used as a raw material for alcohol and a variety of building boards.

Africa has never really exploited the fact that African countries can grow large quantities of crops that can be used as raw materials for their own agro-industry. There is no doubt that Africa can be in a very competitive position in this field, but only if they are willing to mechanize their agriculture and process their own products in modern and highly efficient factories.

The situation is the same in industry. No appropriate technology will produce goods cheaply enough for the international market, even if the salaries are below those of other countries. International aid, however, does not accept or even recognize this simple fact, and instead prolongs the agony of Africa by maintaining, supporting, and promoting unproductive systems, such as small-scale agriculture, village technology, and small, inefficient rural industries.

It all started with the British-financed Land Transfer Scheme, under which some 2 million acres of formally European-owned farmland were divided up into small holdings, frequently into pieces of land of only six hectares. In every country in Africa, aid organizations repeat the mistakes of the British and support land-development schemes similar to the Arid Region Irrigation Development Program in Kenya. There are hundreds of projects such as the Wei-Wei river scheme, by which new, irrigated land is divided up into farms that are too small for modern productive agriculture. This approach, maintained by the national and international aid organizations, is based on the misconception that by dividing the land up, the poor are helped, in spite of the fact that in the long run this policy makes the whole nation sink even deeper in poverty. It is further supported by the African elite, but for purely political reasons. By giving the poor and landless Africans a small piece of land to cultivate, the wealthy politicians in every African capital hope to pacify the dissatisfied masses, whose only aspiration is a piece of land for themselves and not modern, large-scale agriculture.

As with the establishment of small, unproductive farms, a considerable part of all international aid promotes and financially supports the establishment of small industries, which basically are unproductive and therefore uneconomical, such as the Industrial Estates and the Rural Industrial

Development Centers in Kenya, which are financed by GTZ, ODA, and several Scandinavian aid organizations. All this type of aid is in the long run wasted, for small-scale industries will never raise the productivity per man, which is a fundamental requirement for real development. The international aid organizations, with the help of the African elite, who have only political motives, are using huge amounts of money to establish industries of the kind Europe and America had a hundred years ago. By doing this, they fail completely in pursuing the primary target, which can only be to *increase* production to the highest possible level. They do not utilize the basic principle of modern industry: mass production by machines, each performing the work of hundreds of men with great precision at very high speed.

In addition to increasing productivity, Africa must find ways of mobilizing and employing millions of unemployed all over the continent. The curse of Africa is that whenever modernization of African agriculture and industry is planned, the problem of labor-intensive versus mechanized enterprises becomes a controversial issue. The main reason for this dilemma is that Africa has been *forced* to develop modern agriculture and industry, first by the colonials and later by the huge international companies. Africa has therefore embarked on a course completely at odds with the *natural* development of the continent, and the price is paid by creating some of the most artificial societies ever known. It is too late now to reverse this development, return to nature, and embark on a sort of ecologically sound society in Africa.

To modernize agriculture and build a new agro-industry are in principle quite simple with the aid of European and American technology. To mobilize the millions of unemployed is, however, a quite different problem. It is also a problem that only the Africans can solve. Africa must create a new economic, social, and political structure that will make it possible for the millions of squatters around every capital in Africa and the millions streaming into every city in search of work to be employed building roads, water reservoirs, irrigation schemes, and storage depots all over Africa. International aid, however, will not encourage the Africans to do something on their own and, at the moment, is trying to build an infrastructure the Africans are quite capable of building themselves. Africans can build roads, construct dams, and lay down pipes for irrigation and water supplies. But while millions have nothing to do, expensive and modern road-building machinery is paid for by European taxpayers and sent to Africa.

The equipment is never fully utilized. To start with, the equipment is usually delayed at the African docks. It is stored in the open, deteriorating in the tropical sun and rusting in the humid coastal atmosphere. When it is finally put into operation, the breakdowns are numerous, parts are stolen, and maintenance is poor or completely nonexistent. All over Africa, sometimes stored in the port areas, other times found in the government depots, and often just abandoned along the road, road-building machinery, tractors, bulldozers, and trucks sit idle. In spite of this, international aid, especially the British and the Scandinavian variety, seems to be obsessed with the idea of building roads.

The largest single project that Britain has undertaken in Africa is the Songeo-Makambako trunk road in Tanzania at a cost of £39 million. The Rural Access Road Program in Kenya is supported by international and national aid organizations such as UNDP, NORAD, DANIDA, ODA, USAID, and others. In Tanzania, the Norwegian aid program, as part of a large IDA road-building project, is funding 520 kilometers of regional roads in the districts of Rungwe and Lushoto and has provided funds for mobile road-building units and running expenses. In Botswana, money is provided by IDA, Norway, Sweden, Britain, Canada, the U.S., Germany, and other countries to build a network of roads that will make Botswana less dependent upon transport through South Africa. The list is almost without end.

Africans are quite capable of building their own roads. They have enough qualified people in Africa for surveying and planning the roads, and they have millions of idle, unemployed Africans who could provide the labor for building even the most enterprising road system.

The Romans built their road network in the whole of Europe, North Africa, and the Middle East with simple hand tools. They erected some of the most impressive engineering structures in the world with their bare hands. Why can the Africans not do the same? Why can they not take a pick and shovel instead of waiting for some British, Scandinavian, American, or German aid to supply them with tractors and bulldozers and complicated road-building machines? Why must people in Europe and America pay for even the *maintenance* of roads in Africa, which any nation on earth, developed or underdeveloped, is quite capable of doing on its own?

International aid often seems to get everything wrong. When machinery is needed, an unproductive appropriate technology is promoted; and when machinery is detrimental to employment, expensive and complicated machinery is supplied. International aid supports appropriate technology when the only feasible solution is advanced, modern agriculture and industry. It supports the use of mechanized road building when road building is one of the few activities in Africa that with advantage could be made very labor intensive. With every road scraper, bulldozer, and truck off-loaded in Mombasa, Dar es Salaam, and Maputo, many potential jobs are taken away from Africans.

In no other field have the national and international aid organizations shown so little insight and understanding of Africa's problems as in the fields of agriculture, industry, and infrastructure. The UN, the various aid organizations, and the international bureaucracy have failed to understand

and pursue a policy in Africa that should have only one single purpose: to increase productivity in growing, processing, and manufacturing more goods. They could certainly learn from a statement by Lee Iacocca, the then president of Ford Motor Company, given at a meeting of the Swiss-American Chamber of Commerce in Zurich in 1977: "No matter what the social and institutional groundwork is, the key element of development will have to be productivity. There is no alternative, even though that is a subject which is much abused in all theoretical and political discussions of the problems of development."

Africa must produce or perish.

8 / The Obstacles

Even if the African countries do make the right choice for the model of development, manage to increase agriculture and industrial production, and are successful in mobilizing the masses, there are many obstacles ahead, some so serious and of such a magnitude that they may effectively nullify all the efforts of development in Africa. Some of the obstacles are an inherent part of present-day Africa, such as population explosion, rural-to-urban migration, and the change in climatic conditions. Others are introduced to Africa by forces that are alien to the continent, such as Soviet imperialism and the invasion of cheap industrialized products from the East. Any one of the obstacles represents a threat to Africa, and each one could neutralize the continent's own efforts. To be confronted with several of them simultaneously could spell catastrophe.

The Increasing Millions

The population explosion is more serious in Africa than anywhere else in the world. It is not only the *total* increase in population that is a deterrent to effective development, but also the large migration to Africa's expanding cities, which represents an almost insurmountable problem.

The annual growth rate of the population in Africa is one of the highest in the world. In 1977, the average growth rate for the whole of Africa was around 2.6 percent. Many countries in Africa have a higher rate—often approaching 4 percent—than the continent's average. Based on the 1977 growth rate, in twenty-three years' time the total population will increase from about 448 million to about 856 million. If the growth rate rises to 3 percent within the 1980s, which is possible, the population could exceed 900 million by the year 2000 (A. C. G. Best and H. J. de Blij, *African Survey*, John Wiley & Sons, New York, 1977). The incredible magnitude of the growth of Africa's population becomes apparent when one realizes that the world's *total* population in 1850 was only a little more than Africa's will be by the turn of the century. According to H. J. de Blij *Human Geography*, (John Wiley and Sons, New York, 1977) and *Plain Truth* (October/November 1974), the world's total population in 1820 was around 1 billion. The current growth rate of the world population is much below that of Africa. During the century between 1750 and 1850, the growth rate of the world's population was about 0.5 percent; this increased in 1950–75 to an average of 1.9 percent per year (*Scientific American*, special issue on human population, September 1974).

As Best and de Blij have pointed out, all demographic data for Africa must be treated with caution due to incomplete, erroneous, and often highly suspect censuses and surveys. It is nevertheless possible to get an accurate picture of the magnitude of the population explosion in several countries, and there is often a good agreement between the various estimates, as the following examples will show:

• The population in Kenya was 13.8 million in 1976, and the growth rate exceeded 3 percent (Ministry of Overseas Development, U.K.).

- In 1979 Kenya's population was 15.3 million, and the growth rate about 3.9 percent (SIDA).
- Kenya's population was 14.9 million in 1978, and the rate of growth was 3.8 percent per annum during 1970 to 1977 (NORAD).
- Best and de Blij give the population in Kenya as 14.5 million in 1977, with an annual growth rate of 3.3 percent (*African Survey*).

Growth rates of the magnitude given above indicate that Kenya's population will double in eighteen to twenty-one years and that the population at the turn of the century will be around 31 million. Other countries in Africa, like Tanzania, with a growth rate of 3 percent in 1978, have similar rapid increases (ODA). This is confirmed by SIDA and NORAD, which also quote a growth rate of 3 percent. This means that the total population of Tanzania will have grown from 17.5 million in 1978 to about 30 million by the year 2000. In some other countries the population explosion will be even more serious—for example, Nigeria, where there will be 198 million people in the year 2000 compared with 68.5 million in 1975 (*Scientific American*, special issue, September 1974).

Despite these alarming facts, no one seems to take the situation seriously enough. The United Nations has naturally held numerous meetings, and the international bureaucracy has concocted a multitude of schemes and projects for family planning and birth control. In 1974, the UN held a World Population Conference. Delegates from 135 nations met in Bucharest, Rumania, where they naturally accomplished nothing except to make a lot of propaganda for the World Population Year. While the delegates attended the 12-day conference, two million people were added to the world's population (*Plain Truth*, October/November 1974), thereby adding to the misery of those millions who are already starving. The various national and international aid organizations are engaged in family planning all over

Africa, a project just as hopeless and futile as their attempts to increase food production.

Parallel with the increase in Africa's population, millions of Africa's landless and unemployed are streaming into all the big cities on the continent. If the figures for the population explosion are alarming, the statistics for rural-to-urban migration are even more so.

During the first half of October 1978, twenty-seven African countries attended the African Regional Meeting on Human Settlements Finance and Management held in Nairobi. The meeting focused attention on the disturbing fact that the tremendous rural-to-urban migration would cause Africa's urban population to rise from 75 million in 1970 to 333 million by the year 2000 (*Uniterra*, October 1978). An alarming aspect of this is that the large capitals, which already are so terribly overcrowded, grow even faster than the smaller cities, as in the case of Lagos, which had a population of 1.4 million in 1970 but will have 9.4 million by the year 2000 ("The State of the World Population in 1978," UN Fund for Population Activities).

Even now, vast populations in the rural areas are deprived of even the basic human settlement needs, including shelter, clear water, and sanitation.

After considering that in the next twenty years more than 250 million new migrants will have to be accommodated among the teeming millions in African cities, and after realizing that between three and five of every ten urban dwellers in Africa are presently living in squatter areas and without fundamental environmental needs, it is difficult to come to any other conclusion than that it will all end in a major catastrophe.

In view of this, the world's international bureaucracy, represented by United Nations Habitat and Human Settlement Foundation, HABITAT, UNEP, UNDP, USAID, and local government officials, have come up with an answer to Africa's settlement problems that is not only uninspired and without any real meaning, but totally without any practical value. According to one of UNEP's many publications (*Uniterra*, October 1978), "the meeting called on African governments to make far reaching changes in their present process of planning, financing and management of human settlement." While millions live in the overcrowded slums of Africa's cities, and further millions will migrate there, swelling the numbers to a staggering 333 million by the turn of the century, representatives from twenty-seven African countries and half a dozen UN organizations cannot come up with any suggestion other than to urge "far reaching changes" to improve the human settlement conditions in Africa!

There are in reality no solutions to the problems caused by the population explosion in Africa and the huge rural-to-urban migration. Neither the African countries nor the UN and all its organizations have the slightest idea how to stem the tide and to avoid a disaster.

Paul Demeny, the well-known demographic expert, was probably right when he predicted in *Scientific American* (September 1974) that control of the growth of the population in the underdeveloped countries will eventually come through development or catastrophe. At that time, 1974, there was still hope for development. Now growth will be checked only by catastrophe, for efforts to reduce the population explosion in Africa have been in vain.

The population bomb is relentlessly ticking away, but with food production declining, the explosion may come earlier than expected.

The Dwindling Water

Much has been written about the expanding deserts, and millions of dollars have been used to provide water for the arid and semiarid areas of Africa. Every year at regular intervals the world is bombarded with horror stories about droughts, spreading deserts, and famine.

From the beginning of the 1970s the world's mass media

has been full of reports, data, and pictures of deserts on the march, and the starving people and dying cattle.

"The Sahara continues its journey south" (*New Scientist*, October 4, 1973).

"The worst drought of the century" (Cape Town *Cape Times*, October 6, 1973).

"Merciless march of Africa's killer drought" (*Reader's Digest*, August 1974).

"In the Sahel area, the vegetation is drying out, the wells are empty, the cattle is dying and millions of people are threatened with famine" (*Der Spiegel*, August 12, 1974).

"Is the ecological catastrophe already here?" (Oslo *Aftenposten*, August 26, 1975).

"650,000 sq. kilometres of good land has been lost to Saharan sands in the last 50 years" (Cape Town *Argus*, July 27, 1976).

"Deserts on the march in a shrinking world" (Cape Town *Weekend Argus*, July 31, 1976).

"In Sudan, the desert's southern boundary had shifted 100 km to the south" (Cape Town *Argus*, December 8, 1976).

"The creeping deserts: How to beat them" (*New Africa*, July 1977).

"Poor rainfalls in eight Sahel nations have led to renewed drought" (Nairobi *Daily Nation*, January 30, 1978).

The spreading of the desert is a fact, but no one knows if it is a cyclical phenomenon that will reverse in a few years. What we do know, however, is that long ago some of the African deserts had a quite different climate. What is now desert was several thousand years ago rich agricultural land.

Going back far enough in time, it is almost certain that the Sahara was not a vast expanse of sand but a tropical jungle. In the Natural History Museum in Tripoli one can see the bones of a giant mastodon, a herbivorous animal of colossal size. When the animal was alive, it must have had lush vegetation and thick forests as its habitat. Today the same area is part of the Libyan deserts, where practically nothing grows. Not so long ago, in the fifth century B.C., the historian Herodotus wrote that North Africa was equal to any area in the world for cereal crops. The soil of North Africa was so productive that the historian Pliny referred to the area as the granary of the world. Where the Romans had enormous areas under cultivation, there is today nothing but sand and a few oases.

The nations in Africa affected the most are Mauritania, Senegal, Mali, Upper Volta, Niger, Chad, Sudan, Ethiopia, and Somalia. In addition, the northern parts of Uganda, Kenya, and even Tanzania are exposed to severe droughts. In recent years, the drought conditions have also spread to the southern part of Africa in Zimbabwe, Mozambique, Botswana, and South Africa. The gravity of the situation cannot be fully assessed today, for we do not know if in the next years the trend will reverse and rain will return to the land that is now a semidesert. It now seems certain that North Africa gets wetter and the Sahel area gets drier. The whole of the Sahara is moving south—since 1960, this shift has taken place at a rate of nine kilometers a year. The world has undergone similar climatic changes before. If the increase of the desert areas of the Sahel countries is part of the movement of climatic zones in the entire northern hemisphere, the long-term changes are very serious indeed. And if Derek Winstanley is correct—that the decline of rainfall in the Sahel zone since 1960 will probably continue until the year 2030 (Derek Winstanley, *Nature* 245)—there is nothing that can be done to stop the advance of the desert in Africa north of the equator.

The tremendous scale of climatic changes and the incredible number of energy systems involved in periodically or permanently changing climatic zones preclude any possibility that man-made efforts can halt the advancing desert. It is therefore incorrect to say that "thanks largely to man's own folly, desertification now threatens the fragile existence of about 630 million people who dwell in these regions" (*Time*, September 12, 1977). The deserts' advance is due to changes in the radiated energy of the sun, variations in the atmosphere's content of carbon dioxide, and even fluctuations of the magnetic fields of the earth.

The national and international aid organizations are also wrong when they keep alive the myth that financial aid, the drilling of water holes, and the planting of green belts can stop the advance of the deserts. They all promote the impossible, selecting some single project, which is successful until the boreholes run dry, and ignoring the results of the *total* effort, which are always negative.

Take, for example, the German Bundesministerium für Wirtschaftliche Zusammenarbeit (BMZ), which spreads propaganda for aid not only within its own country but throughout the whole world: "We must look after the other half of the world [the Third World] so their deserts are not spreading and destroying our climate." In beautifully prepared publications, which would be a credit to any top-class advertising agency, the public is actually told that if German development aid does not stop the spreading of deserts somewhere else, the climate in Germany will be destroyed! To back up these completely unscientific claims, a single success story is quoted about a small town, Iférouane, at the edge of the Sahara: "With money coming from German development aid in Bonn, water schemes and irrigation projects were carried out. As a result plants were growing where the desert had been, and more cattle and people could live in the area than ever before. In brief: aid is worthwhile."

What the publications from BMZ, or any other national aid organization, will never tell is that aid of this nature prepares the ground for even greater disasters. They never tell the public that a project of this nature in Africa will collapse when the foreign experts finally go home. Installations and equipment will stop functioning because of either misuse, lack of maintenance, or theft of spare parts.

When the inevitable disaster finally strikes, due to an unexpected severe drought or the collapse of dams, canals, water holes, or the breakdown of irrigation equipment, the disaster will be many times more severe because of the millions spent by European taxpayers on a futile project in the Sahara. Where before a few thousand would have been exposed to starvation, tens of thousands of people and huge herds of cattle will suddenly be exposed to terrible conditions, starvation, and death because of the follies of international aid.

The German experiment in Iférouane is being repeated by the British, the Americans, the Dutch, and the Scandinavians in all the arid zones in Africa, where they move in with their drilling rigs, water pumps, concrete mixers, and diesel-driven machinery. And all the national aid organizations will spread success stories like BMZ's. But no one will tell the story when a project collapses, which is the fate of all efforts of this kind in Africa.

We have over a period of many years spoken to international experts from the U.S. and many countries in Europe who have worked in Africa. Without exception, they relate the same experience. The project works only as long as the experts and the aid organizations run the project and operate the equipment. After they have left, there is only one outcome. It may take months or years, but in the end the project will collapse.

About the climates of the world man can do nothing; neither can the 1,500 delegates who gathered in Nairobi in 1977 to take part in a United Nations Conference on Desertification. Among the participating agencies were the UNDP, UNESCO, FAO, WHO (the World Health Organization), and WMO (the World Meteorological Organization).

As at any other UN conference, several plans of action were adopted that, as usual, reflect lack of realism. One speaker after another stood up and proclaimed that the deserts were man-made and their spread could therefore be arrested. So many of the speakers and so many of the conclusions reached at the conference maintained that desertification was seen as a human problem in both its origins and effects.

If the spread of the deserts is part of large variations in the climate, there is no scientific foundation for the conclusion that man can stop the advance of deserts. Occasionally it is possible to halt the deserts at the fringe areas with the planting of green belts and irrigation, but this can be only a temporary measure. If the deserts really are advancing, there is nothing or very little we can do to control desertification. The Assyrians could not do it in Mesopotamia, the Egyptians could not do it in ancient Egypt, and the Romans could not do it in North Africa thousands of years ago. Likewise, no action plan of a UN conference can stop the advancing desert today.

Instead of accepting this, and instead of accepting that the impending catastrophe of climatic changes is already here, the UN conference on desertification raises false hopes for the millions who live in arid or semiarid areas and will soon be engulfed in nothing but sand and barren rocks.

True to the usual UN style of bombastic statements and extravagant claims, UNEP in a 1979 publication (United Nations Environmental Program, Nairobi) congratulates itself with excellent work and states:

Another outstanding example of UNEP's operational style could be taken from the UN Conference on Desertification held in Nairobi in August/September 1977.

The ultimate objective is to sustain and promote, within ecological limits, the productivity of arid, semiarid, subhumid and other areas vulnerable to desertification in order to improve the quality of life of their inhabitants.

The immediate goal of the plan of action to control desertification, adopted by the Conference, is to prevent and arrest the advance of desertification and, where possible, to reclaim desertified land to productive use.

In other words, the conference accepts as possible and prepares plans for preventing and arresting the desertification, thereby presenting a wrong view to the world. With our present technology we cannot prevent or arrest the spread of deserts. The resources we have are minute compared with the enormous energy reservoir contained in the atmosphere. It is not the land masses or the biosphere we are dealing with, but the total changes of energy in the atmosphere and our climate. Man is simply not in the position to take up this fight.

To make small parts of the desert bloom requires irrigation, of which we have many examples in Israel, North Africa, China, and the U.S., but that is a problem quite different from attempting to halt the *spread* of deserts, and is possible only if there is water somewhere in the neighborhood that can be pumped from natural underground reservoirs or transported via pipes or canals from rivers or lakes.

Even the enormous water reservoirs under the Sahara can be used only for cultivation of limited areas and not for halting the Sahara's advance in the Sahel countries. To stop any desert from spreading is therefore not feasible within the foreseeable future with the resources we have today, but we can learn to live with the desert as the nomads have done for thousands of years.

The nomads, not only of Africa but of all continents, have established an ecological equilibrium with nature which they are using to the fullest. The nomads have lived with the desert, become part of it, and exploited its few riches. From the Kalahari in the south to the Libyan desert in the north, the nomads have survived in the desert for thousands of years by following the simple principle of constantly being on the move with their herds to new pastures and new water holes in accordance with the yearly changes in climate and vegetation. The Bedouins in the

Sahara wander freely over vast areas of desert with the one animal that makes such a life possible, the camel. The Hamitic tribes of the northeastern Sudan make yearly treks through the valleys of the Red Sea hills. The cattle breeders move south and back north with the seasonal changes of the weather. Sometimes the nomads stay in the wadis of the desert for longer periods, but otherwise they are constantly on the move. Each year they travel long distances with their herds of camels, goats, and cattle, not haphazardly but according to a pattern and a timetable it took generations to develop.

The life of the nomads would have continued for many more generations to come if it had not been for the impact of international aid invading almost every country in Africa. With aid came the drilling rigs. Soon water holes were drilled by the thousands, and only national or international aid organizations could take pride in having bored as many water holes as possible. The policy of providing water to the nomadic people of Africa soon upset the delicately balanced equilibrium between nature, man, and beast.

According to the well-known expert on Africa Basil Davidson: "Aid for development accentuated a growth that could be crippling in its consequences. Flocks and herds in the Sudanese Sahel, were enlarged by a multiplication of water points without any rational plan of long-term conservation and ecological balance" (*Africa in Modern History*, Pelican Books, New York, 1978).

Claire Sterling underlines some of the most dangerous results of drilling water holes in the Sahel district without any real plan or understanding of the laws of the desert and the heritage of the nomads: "Carried away by the promise of unlimited water, nomads forgot about the Sahel's all-too-limited forage, and centuries-old tribal agreements that apportioned just so many cattle to graze just so long in just so many districts, were brushed aside. Enormously increasing herds, converging on the new boreholes from hundreds of kilometres away, so ravaged the surrounding land by trampling and overgrazing that each borehole quickly became the centre of its own little desert, 30 to 60 kilometres in square. After they had drunk all they liked, the cattle could no longer make it back to any remaining pasture. They died, not of thirst, but of hunger" ("Merciless March of Africa's Killer Drought," *Reader's Digest*, August 1974.

The influence of European and American civilizations upset the natural balance in the arid areas, not only by the boring of thousands of water holes, but by ruining the nomads' traditional way of life. To the newly independent African governments, the nomads are an embarrassment. Seen as primitive people who do not want to belong to the general development of their nations, everything possible is done to "settle" the nomads. This is widely encouraged by national and international aid organizations. Every year they spend huge sums of money to build roads, training centers, and schools for the nomads, hoping they will settle down and stop roaming around in the desert. The result is that the nomads, who were enormously suited to a life in the desert, degenerate and lose their ability to survive under the extreme, dry climatic conditions, as David Etherton points out in *Shelter in Africa* (Barrie and Jenkins, London, 1971).

The nomads have seen Phoenician, Roman, Byzantine, Arab, and Turkish domination of North Africa without his way of life being upset, but what the world powers through the centuries never attempted to do is now carried out in defiance of the law of nature. What national and international aid can supply in temporary relief, such as food and medicine, is completely offset by the long-term effect their aid programs have on the people living in the arid and desert regions in the Sahel countries and neighboring areas.

The United Nations has more ambitious plans than

stopping the advance of the desert and drilling water holes for the nomads and their animals. They will concentrate on providing water for the whole world during the International Drinking Water Supply and Sanitation Decade (1981–90).

The idea of providing safe drinking water to all people in the world was originally suggested at the HABITAT conference in Vancouver, Canada, in 1976, and later recommended by the United Nations Water Conference in Mar del Plata, Argentina, in 1977, and a WHO–UNICEF international meeting in Alma-Ata, Russia, in 1978. Like everything else the UN does, providing water for the world's thirsty is seen as merely a question of money. WHO and the World Bank have estimated that $140 billion will be needed during the ten-year period. The immense program for the water decade is only in its infancy, but Dr. Halfdan Mahler, director-general of WHO, indicated at a press briefing on November 10, 1981, that to solve the world's problem of water scarcity, $50 million per day would be needed!

If the nomads in the arid areas of Africa could be left in peace and their traditional way of life preserved, they would survive as they have done for thousands of years. To supply water to the rest of Africa, where water supplies are often plentiful, is only a question of administration and engineering. In almost every country where there is a drought, as is the present difficult situation in northern Kenya and Uganda, the problems are not really insurmountable because there is plenty of water in other parts of the country. It is a question of a distribution of water and sometimes a redistribution of an entire population group.

Another obstacle to the development of a free, independent Africa is quite different from those inherent to the continent itself. This is the threat of the last imperialists, represented by the colonial aspirations of the U.S.S.R. and the Communist bloc.

The Red Menace

After the old empires in Africa collapsed, and after colonial rule was dismantled, an entirely new imperial power appeared on the scene, that of the Soviet Union and its satellite countries in East Europe. While the greatest empires in our history, the Roman and the British, were military, economic, and cultural undertakings and conquered the greatest part of the known world for the purpose of using the new land as colonies, the Soviet empire is obsessed with spreading the philosophy of world revolution. Little has changed since Lenin sat in Zurich in 1916 and wrote his publications about imperialism and capitalism: "Monopolies, oligarchy, the striving for domination and not for freedom, the exploitations of an increasing number of small or weak nations by a handful of the richest or most powerful nations, all these have given birth to those distinctive characteristics of imperialism which compels us to define it as parasitic or decaying capitalism" (*Imperialism, the Highest Stage of Capitalism*, Progress Publishers, Moscow, 1978).

Sixty years later the world is told by Leonid Breshnev, the current leader of world Communism: "The recent experience of the revolutionary movement provides graphic evidence that imperialism will stop at nothing, discarding all semblance of any kind of democracy, if serious threats arise to the domination of monopoly capital and its political agents. It is prepared to trample upon the sovereignty of states and upon all legality, to say nothing about humanism. Slander, duping the public, economic blockade, sabotage, bringing about hunger and dislocation, bribes and threats, terrorism, assassination of political leaders, and fascist-style pogroms. Such is the armoury of present-day counterrevolution, which always operates in conjunction with international imperialists reaction (Documents and Resolutions, XXV Congress of the CPSU, Moscow, 1976).

The outspoken denunciation of imperialism, as articulated by Lenin, has not changed in character for the last sixty
years but has only grown in intensity and animosity against
the world the Communists call capitalistic and imperialistic. Breshnev's string of accusations against imperialism,
which he holds responsible for all the world's evil, has been
heard a thousand times before and will be repeated a
thousand times again. No other nation on earth has
matched the U.S.S.R. in its never-ending propaganda of
hatred against the rest of the world.

They spread their message of hatred, their gospel of
world revolution, and their animosity against Western
democracies over hundreds of powerful radio transmitters
and in hundreds of newspapers and thousands of publications in all the languages of the world. It is disseminated to
the farthest corners of the world, day and night, around the
clock, year after year.

Whenever a shot is fired in Africa—in a civil war, when
black is killing black, or in a struggle between white and
black—the Soviet Union will have been involved one way
or the other. Their Kalashnikovs, their Degtyarevs, their
landmines, and their MiGs will kill people all over Africa.
Whether innocent people are blown to pieces by landmines
in Namibia, terrorists kill civilians in South Africa, or
Ethiopians bomb villages in Eritrea and Somalia, the Soviet
hardware of destruction makes it all possible. The slaughter
of tens of thousands of blacks and whites in Mozambique,
Angola, Rhodesia, and Uganda is made possible because
the rulers of the U.S.S.R. believe anything is permissible
in their struggle against "world imperialism and monopolis-
tic capitalism." They supply all the weapons, and the
indoctrination does the rest.

Since the time of Lenin, they have preached only one
thing, believed in only one thing, and acted as if there was
only one truth: imperialism is the last stronghold of capitalism, and the promotion of world revolution is the only
salvation. In the end, the leaders inside the thick walls of the

Kremlin have become prisoners of their own sterile philosophy and victims of their own dogmatic propaganda.

As Solzhenitsyn has so often pointed out, the Communist leaders of the U.S.S.R. preach a philosophy and have developed a political system that will continue to exist only as long as they expand their influence and power. The very nature of the system is aggressive, and with the development of a modern technological society in the U.S.S.R., they now have the physical means to spread their power and influence all around the world. Soviet imperialism is therefore an inevitable result of their policy of domination and an unavoidable conclusion to their philosophy.

Until a few years ago, it was technically possible to keep only Eastern Europe occupied and under their rule. Now, with the advent of the very advanced technology of air and sea transport, it is possible for the U.S.S.R. to expand its military operations to Africa. Not that the desire for world conquest is a new one, but until they could safely get into Africa with their huge fleet of Ilyushin and Antonov transport planes, a direct military intervention in Africa was impossible. The V-TA, the transport section of the Soviet air force can now send its huge Il-76s and An-22s, laden with men, weapons, and ammunition, from bases in the Ukraine near the Black Sea all the way down Africa to Angola and Ethiopia.

Like so many other political and military developments in history, the appearance of the U.S.S.R. as an imperial power in Africa—and elsewhere—has been made possible by the development of new technology. In addition to being able to cross the African continent with their fleet of transport planes, the Soviet navy can now control most of the seaways around Africa. From Aden in the north to Maputo on the east coast and Luanda on the west coast, the Soviet navy can dock, fuel, and repair their Kresta-class missile cruisers, Moskva-class helicopter cruisers, and Krivak-class frigates while its Minsk- and Kiev-class aircraft carriers are patrolling the Atlantic and Indian oceans. At the same time, the Soviet navy is supplying Mozambique and Angola with smaller strike craft. Every week the South African air force brings in photographs of Soviet freighters, their decks crammed with military equipment. Every month, ships from the Far Eastern Shipping Company in Vladivostok, such as the freighter *Olga*, are photographed with such deck cargo as the Turya-class torpedo boats.

There can be no doubt about the offensive character of the transport section of the Soviet air force, the V-TA. Neither is there any doubt about the offensive capabilities of the Soviet navy, a fact clearly underlined by the Soviet admiral Sergei Gorshkov, who declares that "the Soviet Navy is a powerful factor in the creation of favourable conditions for the building of socialism and Communism, for the active defence of peace and for strengthening international security" (*The Soviet War Machine*, Salamander Books, London, 1980). As the Soviet Navy is hardly required to build socialism and Communism *inside* the U.S.S.R., it is obvious it is designed to "defend peace and international security" somewhere else. And where Admiral Gorshkov's philosophy is already being carried out is in the sea lanes around Africa.

While the West can do nothing to counteract the Soviet expansion in Africa, the U.S.S.R. is busy building up an important prerequisite for any colonial or imperialistic power: the means for transport by sea and air and the possession of the necessary military hardware to protect its transport routes. Already Mozambique, Angola, and Ethiopia are under direct influence of the U.S.S.R. Tanzania, Zambia, and Zimbabwe are trying to create a sort of African socialism and are sympathetic to the Soviet influence in Africa. In light of the Soviet military build-up in southern Africa, there can be no doubt that the last target for the Soviet expansion is South Africa. Mozambique has a pact of friendship with the U.S.S.R., which requires that Soviet forces come to their assistance in case of an external threat. Such threats can be imaginery, as in the case of the Soviet invasion of Afghanistan.

In January 1981 South African commandos carried out a raid in Matola near Maputo that was used as an excuse for the appearance of four Soviet warships in Maputo and Beira after a request from President Samora Machel (Johannesburg *Financial Mail*, February 27, 1981). Occasions like this can be an excuse for any intervention by the U.S.S.R. in southern Africa.

The world did nothing about the Soviet intervention in Angola and Ethiopia, and very little after Afghanistan was invaded. What can the world do if Machel asks the U.S.S.R. to intervene in any conflict between South Africa and Mozambique? The world will do nothing in this case, for a conflict will result in the downfall of apartheid in South Africa. The leaders in the Kremlin know this, and they are playing a dangerous game in brinkmanship, which so often before has brought the world to the edge of disaster. The war by proxy, which gave such good results in Angola and Mozambique, may be tried again in Mozambique against South Africa.

The red menace is a real one, and could put an end to all development of a free, independent Africa. No one has earnestly tried to stop the Soviet expansion in Africa. On the contrary, many countries in Europe have supported every Marxist or Marxist-imposed guerrilla movement in Africa in their fight for supremacy in Mozambique, Angola, Rhodesia, Namibia, and South Africa. The Western world has made every Soviet move in Africa an easy one, and they have prepared everything for the last onslaught on South Africa.

Only time will tell if the U.S.S.R. can resist the temptation to take a final calculated risk to rule the whole of southern Africa, either directly or by proxy. The West has allowed South Africa to become a *soft option* for the Soviet expansion in Africa, and one day they will have to pay a high price for this lack of courage and determination.

9 / Maintaining the Illusion

In spite of the increasing criticism of international aid, especially from the U.S., England, and Germany, there is nothing to indicate that the almost pathological symptom of the aid syndrome—the mania for meetings and conferences —is diminishing. On the contrary, the United Nations and the international bureaucracy have realized that the only way they can maintain the illusion that international aid works is by increasing the number of international meetings and conferences.

Because the international bureaucracy is immune to criticism and because there is no other yardstick for their activities and accomplishments than the number and size of their conferences, the conference mania will be nurtured and maintained as if it were a question of life and death. In one way it is, since the increasing number of meetings and conferences can be used to maintain another illusion: that a huge bureaucracy is required to plan, organize, and take part in all the activities of politicians and world leaders when they get together in faraway and often exotic places around the world.

It is totally impossible for one person to keep track of all the meetings and conferences organized to keep politicians, aid experts, and the international bureaucracy busy, but some of the meetings acquire such proportions or pretend to be so impressive that they deserve a closer analysis. Some of the recent ones that fall in this category are: the United Nations Conference on New and Renewable Sources of Energy, in Nairobi (August 10–21, 1981), the United Nations Conference on the Least Developed Countries in Paris (September 1–14, 1981), and the International Meeting on Cooperation and Development, in Cancún (October 22–23, 1981). These meetings are of special interest for the development in Africa, and are therefore dealt with in some detail in the following.

The Nairobi Conference

About 3,000 participants from 125 countries met in Nairobi in August 1981 to discuss the world's energy problem, with special emphasis on the poor and developing countries. Representatives from 101 nations made statements in the general debate about their own energy problems and advised other countries how they should cope with their problems. In addition, twenty-four UN agencies and twelve intergovernmental organizations took part in the mammoth conference.

As usual the main objectives of the conference promised everything: "The central task of the conference will be to come up with a program of action to help provide the world with a sustained, diversified and permanent energy base."

After the conference had heard the inaugural speech by the president of Kenya, Daniel arap Moi, and listened to the then UN secretary-general, Kurt Waldheim; the prime minister of India, Indira Gandhi; the prime minister of Canada, Pierre Trudeau; the prime minister of Sweden, Thorbjørn Fälldin; and others who knew nothing about energy, the secretary-general of the conference, Enrique Iglesias, opened the meeting and stressed that the conference would be both technical and political.

Political it certainly was. Before the 5,000 delegates could discuss energy for the poor, they had to listen to those for whom hatred against their neighbors was more important than the solution to the world's energy problems. First, the obligatory denunciation of Israel was not to be forgotten; the conference condemned Israel for planning to build a canal between the Mediterranean and the Dead Sea. Then international capitalism and South Africa also got their share of condemnation, and the conference adopted a resolution accusing multinational corporations and South Africa for the plunder and illegal exploitation of Namibia's energy resources.

After Iraq, Morocco, Pakistan, and others had found an outlet for their animosity against other nations, the conference finally settled down to discuss how to solve the world's energy problems.

Everyone used the new fashionable words, like solar energy, geothermal hot spots, oil shale, biomass, and many others. Every important northern European politician remotely connected with energy seemed to have found his way to the Kenyatta Conference Center and the luxury hotels of Nairobi. Every one of them had prepared a speech or had had one written, which they solemnly presented to the conference as if they had something new to offer.

The technologies that were discussed varied from the most sophisticated solar panels to simple charcoal stoves. Everyone promoted his own theories about new energies, and as usual, the followers of appropriate, or village, technology advocated their solution as the only one for Africa.

The main problem when thousands of delegates come together for meetings and hundreds give speeches is that in the end no one really knows what it is all about. Very often the confusion is so widespread, that no one can come to a definite conclusion. This conference was in this respect like all the others. They all talked about energy, but no one seemed to discuss what the energy should be used for in developing countries in Africa and the rest of the Third World. To answer that question, there has to be agreement about the meaning of development.

The most important problem of energy for the developing world is, therefore, not simply to provide the energy but to understand and to come to an agreement about the most basic and fundamental issue of development. Until we have defined exactly what type of development is envisaged for Africa and the rest of the Third World, it is futile to discuss new energy resources.

If by development we mean a transition from primitive societies to the type of technologically advanced countries we have in Europe and the United States the answer is simple: Africa will need the same type and the same amount of energy as that used in the industrialized world. Africa and the Third World will then need to build electric power stations based on energy from waterfalls, the burning of coal, and the fission of nuclear material. Some of the countries may not have coal, but they all have hydropower and could acquire nuclear power stations. This, however, is not a problem of energy, but a problem of choosing the right model for development.

If the final target for Africa is to develop like Europe and America, the types of energy dealt with at the conference are of little interest. No one can develop a modern technological society based on the new sources of energy that were discussed for almost two weeks in Nairobi.

With the present technology for alternative energy resources, it is futile even to discuss the use of solar, wind, ocean, geothermal, biomass, charcoal, peat, and draught-animal energy if the African countries want to catch up with the development of Europe and America. Not one of the alternative energy sources discussed in Nairobi can now be used *instead* of energy from hydropower, coal, and nuclear reactors. One day, solar and geothermal energy will provide all of us with sufficient energy, but Africa and the rest of the Third World must solve their energy problems long before such sophisticated energy resources become generally available.

If on the other hand, development of Africa means only the use of appropriate technology, many of the energy resources discussed at the conference have some application. But even then, many of them remain scientific curiosities or gadgets. The energy conference in Nairobi repeated the mistakes of similar meetings before, and concentrated on alternative types of energy that are still in experimental stages or are too expensive to use.

At every meeting on energy for the developing world, including the conference in Nairobi, the inevitable demonstration of a solar reflector and decomposing manure, which produces biogass, takes place. The most these gadgets can accomplish is to warm some water or boil a pot of tea, but they cannot solve a modern nation's energy problem.

This muddled thinking was reflected in the program of action, a sort of conclusion published at the end of all international UN conferences. The preliminary draft for a program of action contained seventy-seven pages and an appendix full of the usual UN jargon, incomprehensible language, and ambiguous statements.

All United Nations conferences have one thing in common. They accept programs of action that are completely unrealistic, beyond the resources and manpower available. The energy conference in Nairobi was no exception. One sentence makes certain that the world's scientists and technologists in the field of energy will be kept busy for the rest of the century: "The programme recommends that a process should now be set in motion to ensure the most efficient identification, explanation, assessment, development and utilization of energy sources, including new and renewable sources of energy." Thus, somebody somewhere in the world has to carry out scientific and technical projects that are many times larger than the combined efforts of the Manhattan and Apollo projects in the U.S.

How does anyone who took part in the Nairobi meeting imagine such a project, which in its scope and immensity exceeds anything else ever undertaken nationally or internationally, can be carried out? Equally unrealistic is the following recommendation by the conference: "To support efforts of all countries to bring about maximum feasible development of new and renewable sources of energy, taking special account of the stage of development reached in the various technologies and of their socio-cultural and environmental impact."

One of the main problems with conferences of this magnitude is that they deal with technical and scientific problems that are basically very different. The building of safe nuclear power stations is a problem quite different from that of growing enough firewood for Africa's starving millions. The experts in the one field cannot even talk intelligently to the experts in the other. A physicist or nuclear engineer has nothing in common with a biologist or forester, and the one cannot discuss separation of radioisotopes or the planting of seedlings with the other.

Added to this is the disturbing fact that most of the delegates to the Nairobi conference were politicians, administrators, and bureaucrats with no real knowledge of energy, whether it comes from splitting atoms or burning wood.

Nothing tangible, almost in principle, can come from conferences of this size and composition, and as expected by many, the conference accomplished very little. To most Africans, who want results now, the two-week discussion in Nairobi achieved nothing. International conferences of this kind serve only to turn the Africans against those who are supposed to help them.

The industrialized countries are therefore being accused of creating the energy problems of the Third World, as stated by President arap Moi at the conference: "It is the profligate use of energy by the rich to support life styles erroneously described as development, that has caused an energy crisis."

Mammoth conferences like the one on energy may look impressive but are in fact of little value. They provide the perfect arena for political showmanship, impressive speeches, and bold promises. The Nairobi meeting also provided the perfect setting for the then UN Secretary-General Kurt Waldheim and Prime Minister Pierre Trudeau to be photographed on the steps of the conference center with tree seedlings, as a contribution to Africa's firewood crisis. And one of the richest men in the world, Prince Aga Khan, was given the opportunity to demonstrate how to cook on a new type of wood-burning stove.

This no longer impresses the Africans. *Africa* magazine's comment (no. 123, 1981) that "the developing world has a good reason to feel bitter about the Nairobi conference" reflects what the Third World thinks about the efforts of one of the United Nations largest and most ambitious meetings.

The euphoric statement by the secretary-general of the Nairobi conference that "the conference was one in which the international community had achieved a new summit in international cooperation" is not a reflection of the Africans feeling about the conference. Nor is it the truth. The conference was a failure, and it would have been much better for international cooperation and the Africans' faith in the industrialized world if the conference had never taken place.

The Paris Conference

The United Nations held a conference in Paris September 1–14, 1981, to discuss the problems of the so-called Least Developed Countries (LDCs) in which 142 countries participated. The Paris conference was a follow-up to UNCTAD V held in Manila in 1979, where an Immediate

Action Program was called for. The Manila meeting also agreed about a project with the somewhat unusual title of a Substantial New Program of Action, which should last until the end of this decade.

The secretary-general of the Paris conference was Gamani Corea, who shares with Tanzania's Julius Nyerere the world record in demanding more money from the industrialized countries. The Paris conference was the ideal setting in which to ask for more money than ever before, for it dealt with the problems of the world's poorest nations.

The inaugural address was given by the president of France, Francois Mitterrand, who promised that France would make up for her past weak performance (note that to give away the nation's tax money is referred to as "performance") by increasing her international aid to 0.7 percent of the GNP by 1988.

The omnipresent Kurt Waldheim, opening the conference, repeated what we all know about poverty, health, hunger, housing, education, and employment and reiterated the only solution known to the United Nations: the transfer of resources and international support must be increased.

The United Nations's obsession in dividing the world into imaginary groups, or constellations, is quite useful as an excuse for expanding their activities in all spheres. They have already created the concepts of the developing world and the developed world, the industrialized world and the Third World, the East and the West, and the North and the South. As if this is not enough, they have invented and taken very seriously another group of countries: The Least Developed Countries.

In a publication issued by the United Nations before the Paris conference, the LDCs are defined: "The Least Developed Countries are not a group of countries that are physically, politically or historically similar, but they have in common the bleak fact of poverty, and this is their main defining characteristic."

As early as 1971, the UN General Assembly defined the LDCs by three criteria:
- a per-capita gross domestic product (GDP) of $100 or less (this limit has since been raised),
- manufacturing accounting for 10 percent or less of the GDP, and
- a literacy rate of 20 percent or less.

Based on these completely arbitrary definitions, the world is now divided in yet another pair: the developing countries and the least developed. At the moment, the UN has designated thirty-one countries as LDCs, of which the majority are in Africa. This suits the international bureaucracy because it is now possible to hold *two* series of meetings on development issues: one on the not-so-poor countries and another on the very poorest ones.

Such a distinction is without justification, for there are many different reasons why many countries in different parts of the world are poor.

It is doubtful if countries like Botswana in Africa, the Yemen Arab Republic in the Middle East, and Haiti in the Caribbean are poor because of some common denominator. In fact, these countries are as different as they could possibly be, but they happen to share some statistical data, which as such are not a reflection of their desire or ability to develop.

It is a cardinal error of the United Nations to lump these countries together and to discuss their problems as if they were different from all other countries. Much that had already been said at every UNCTAD meeting on international aid was repeated at the Paris conference on the LDCs. Several excuses were nevertheless found for dealing with the LDCs as separate issues, and in the report by the secretary-general of the conference it was stressed that "The needs of the poorest and weakest countries are, in any event, particularly acute. Major steps to begin to solve their problems should not wait for the outcome of long negotiations in the framework of the North-South dialogue."

At the same time the secretary-general wanted to make it clear that the other developing countries should get their share of attention: "However, one should beware of using the adoption of a substantial New Program of Action for the LDCs as a pretext for inaction with regard to the other developing countries."

One important aspect of the LDCs that was not discussed at the Paris conference—indeed, a problem that is never discussed by the United Nations—is the ability of all developing countries to really utilize the huge amounts of aid given to them. No one seriously discussed the possibility that the LDCs were poor because they were unable to develop irrespective of the amount of aid given.

On the contrary, true to the tradition of the United Nations, the secretary-general of the conference blamed others for the lack of development, and failed completely to put the responsibility on those countries' own political leaders: "If indeed the LDCs are the product of the mal-development generated by the existing international economic order, the importance of a Substantial New Program of Action for the least developed countries to the whole of the International Development Strategy for the 1980s becomes evident."

As in almost every UN meeting during the last four years, the New International Economic Order is brought up as an answer to all evil. The Paris conference was no exception: "The Substantive New Program of Action will result in a better partnership in development, from which all partners should benefit. Conceived as such it will be an important step towards the establishment of a new international economic order."

Every UN conference is in principle a success, and Kurt Waldheim repeated what was said about almost any international conference sponsored by the UN and its affiliate organizations: "The high level of representation at the conference was a measure of the expectations and support of the international community."

As usual, self-praise was repeated at the final plenary sessions: "A wide-ranging program was approved which was designed to transform the economics of the least developed countries towards sustained self-development and enable them to provide, at least, internationally accepted minimum standards of nutrition, health, housing and education as well as job opportunities to all their citizens, particularly to the rural and urban poor."

One may well ask how representatives of 142 countries at the Paris conference can come together and propose a program that will provide not only minimum standards for all human activities in housing and education but also job opportunities for *all* their citizens when not a single country in Europe or North America can do so for *all* their own citizens!

Such statements reflect dreams, wishful thinking, and pure utopianism. Maybe the participants at the conference believe their own promises, but they do not fool the Africans. The deceit no longer works. As the authoritive *Africa* magazine commented in November 1981: "The world's 31 least developed countries, many of which are on the verge of bankruptcy, went to Paris in September to a major UN conference to discuss their plight. All they received was a document, a so-called substantial new programme of action which is substantial only in words."

The United Nations and other international organizations have lost their grip on the situation in Africa and have failed to accept the facts as they really are. For many years they have kept up the oral battles as a sort of sport for politicians and international bureaucrats. The conference halls were the place they could impress the international community and their own national governments.

The time for empty promises is over, and any more conferences like the one in Paris or the one that followed later in Cancún, can only aggravate the situation. The United Nations and the international bureaucracy are morally bankrupt. And the African knows it. The main question is how long it will be before the taxpayers in Europe and the U.S., who foot the bill, also will accept the African verdict of the Paris conference: "Empty words for the least developed" (*Africa*, November 1981).

The Cancún Meeting

In the introduction to the Report of the Independent Commission on International Development Issues, which we have referred to several times, the chairman, Willy Brandt, suggested that "a summit conference might substantially advance the efforts of the international community to solve the most urgent problems. This should include joint responsibility in the fields of energy and commodities, of finance and jobs, but also a global enterprise to overcome the worst aspects of world hunger and malnutrition by the year 2000."

In the same report, under a proposed program of priorities, a summit of world leaders was outlined in some detail, with the hope "that a summit could enable political leaders to take the first step towards committing themselves and their people to a global agreement for the benefit of the whole world."

To achieve this noble goal, the members of the commission believed that the world leaders would come to a summit meeting where "initiative and concessions should be thrashed out with candour and boldness."

As a result of these recommendations, an international meeting did in fact take place in Cancún, Mexico, on October 22–23, 1981. At an invitation of Mexican President Lopez Portillo, leaders of eight industrial powers and fourteen developing countries came together for two days at the sumptuous Mexican resort of Cancún—a setting that, in all its luxury and glamour, was almost macabre in relation to the main purpose of the meeting: to find means to relieve the miseries of the world's 800 million people who live in absolute poverty. According to one correspondent, the delegates who "feasted on cold avocado cream, grilled lobster and fillet in champagne sauce, and drank Chablis and champagne, saw no Third World poverty" (*Observer*, October 25, 1981).

Instead, the two-day conference was held at the Sheraton —the conference table alone had been made at a cost of $250,000—and the delegates posed happily on the white beaches studded with gleaming hotels and condominiums, against a backdrop of beautiful blue tropical sea.

A lot was expected from the meeting and the *New York Times* (October 22, 1981) therefore wrote "The summit can breathe humanity into dry discussions of dull statistics" and "can stimulate a more effective attack on the poverty that scars and darkens too much of the globe."

If by humanity one means congenial and pleasant surroundings, the conference was a success, but if by effective attacks on poverty one means concrete plans for development, the conference was a total failure. The meeting had no special agenda, and after a few hours' discussion under the chairmanship of Canada's Pierre Trudeau, the leaders failed even to agree on a program of talks. After that, it was a free-for-all, with speeches from the delegates about things nearest to their heart.

President Ronald Reagan reiterated what he had said before—that unless a nation puts its own financial and economic house in order, no amount of aid will produce progress. He also stressed the importance of the American-style free-enterprise system, and proposed to send some of America's experts on agriculture to the Third World to teach them how to grow food.

The British and the Germans backed up the American demands that further negotiations should take place outside the United Nations.

Third World leaders insisted upon implementing a New International Economic Order under the auspices of the international organizations, where they are in the majority.

France, as usual, went her own way and did not agree with anyone else and was adamant about setting up a new energy organization.

Tanzania's President Julius Nyerere repeated what he had said so many times before—that international aid must be increased in spite of the support of $700 million he already gets every year.

The president of the Ivory Coast told the conference what has been said at every meeting on international aid—that Africa needs stable minimum prices for the continent's export products.

Japan's Deputy Foreign Minister stressed that the Communist form of collective agriculture will always produce failure.

At the end of the meeting, no communique was issued and no formal statements were made. Instead, a summary by the cochairmen of the meeting was issued on October 23, reiterating the obvious:

- It was recognized that many of the problems were deep and complex and not subject to quick or simple solutions.
- The importance of strengthening and increasing the effectiveness of cooperation among developing countries was seen as an element of growing significance in international relations.

The cochairmen of the meeting also looked into the future and came up with the following encouragement to a world that had followed the progress in Cancún with interest and even some hope: "Our task will now be to ensure that we build upon this trust and understanding, carry this momentum forward into the future, and translate thought into action and progress with the aid of revolutionizing the world economy and accelerating the development of developing countries."

The meeting accomplished nothing, and even failed for the first time in the history of international bureaucracy, to agree about another meeting! The only concrete result of the Cancún summit was that the world has become more aware of the fact that the so-called world leaders are completely unable to lead the poor and backward countries out of their poverty and misery, a fact that was echoed on October 26, 1981, when the British Parliament condemned the outcome of the Cancún summit as "a cruel and mocking anticlimax to millions of people."

10 / Will Africa Survive?

Africa's difficulties are very serious indeed, probably more serious than people in Europe and America realize. Africa will struggle for mere survival if its main problems are not solved and the main obstacles overcome in the very near future. Things have gone wrong, often irreparably so, and there is very little time left to improve the situation.

Practically all the difficulties Africa is encountering stem from the fact that the Africans have been forced into a development that is not of their own choice. What takes place in Africa today has never been experienced by any other continent before, and what the Western world tries to impose on Africa may be an impossibility. It is against all laws of nature to compress centuries into decades. Maybe it cannot be done.

No one has expressed this so clearly as Dr. Bruno Bandulet in his excellent book on international aid and Africa: "In theory, Africa could have developed harmoniously if the Africans gradually had come into contact with the civilization of the Western world and if they were given a hundred or even two hundred years to become familiar with the technology and science of the West" (Schnee für Afrika [Snow for Africa], Herbig, München & Berlin, 1979).

Dr. Bandulet accepts that in principle Africa can develop as the Western world, but only if given enough time, which in his opinion amounts to one or two hundred years!

The Africans have never been given the opportunity to develop according to their concept of time and according to their natural capacity to cope with development, and therefore the most artificial and unnatural forms of society are now found all over Africa. As a result, the continent is in a state of confusion, both mentally and physically, while the international community does its very best to add to the disorder. But the huge international and national aid organizations have built into their system a mechanism for their own destruction.

The introduction of modern medicine, the building of hospitals, the supply of almost unlimited amounts of curative and preventative medicines, these combined with the huge supplies of imported food have made the population explosion possible. International aid has destroyed the natural equilibrium in Africa between the number of born and the number of surviving and created the highest population explosion in the world.

The tremendous increase in the population has almost nullified any beneficial effect of international aid. With the present population growth in Africa, it is impossible for international aid to increase their aid in proportion to the increase of the population in most of Africa's countries. If aid to Africa is to be maintained at its present level in relation to Africa's increasing population, aid from Europe to Africa must be doubled within the next eighteen to twenty-one years! The donor countries' capacity to increase aid and extract more money from their taxpayers is, after all, limited. Even now, when Europe and the U.S. are confronted with their own serious economic problems, the extent of aid—the six most important donor countries give about 0.75 percent of their gross national products to developing countries—is becoming a difficult burden for many countries. With a serious prospect of 25 million unemployed in Europe, an increase in aid to Africa seems out of the question.

There has been a slow but steady increase of aid from the most important donor countries in Europe (see Appendix), but there are indications that many countries have now (1980–81) reached their limit. While international aid will probably level off, the increase in the population in the countries receiving aid will continue at an alarming rate well into the next century (see Apendix).

International aid has become a monster that no one can control. Neither is there any control over the result of their activities in Africa. Like a dinosaur, it will grow until it becomes so large that it will destroy itself. The conflict, which is built into the international aid organizations as an inherent part of the system, will eventually put an end to the type of aid we know today. The chain reaction of aid, by which aid creates conditions in Africa that demand more aid, will dry up the components that feed the process. Such aid is doomed. To support an accelerating process of this kind is beyond the capacity of Europe and the United States.

International aid has created its own conditions for growth and has maintained the myth for an enormous resource transfer as a condition for development in Africa. As a result, it has created a continent that grows but does not develop. It is growth that neither Africa nor international aid can maintain, a growth that nobody can regulate or stop.

Further efforts from the main donor countries in Europe —and these efforts will be desperate in view of Europe's own 25 million unemployed—can only accentuate and accelerate the final catastrophe. A further increase of the components on which the chain reaction feeds will reduce the chances for survival. Like any chemical or biological reaction that speeds to its own destruction, the important reactant must be taken out of the reaction. Here the reactant is international aid.

There is no other way. Africa must be left alone. Africa must solve her own problems. For thousands of years Africans have relied only on themselves and managed. If they are now to survive, they must rely on themselves again.

Left to themselves, they will pass through one crisis after the other, but they will survive—at a price. If, however, Europe and the U.S. continue in their efforts to change Africa into an image of their own world, insist upon interfering, and are adamant about further increased aid, the Africans will pay a much higher price—indeed, so high that a genuine, lasting survival is in doubt.

Epilogue

International aid concerns us all. As taxpayers, we all are responsible for paying the billions that our governments give to Africa and the Third World every year. In the U.S. and Europe, millions are working to provide the huge amounts of money given away as international aid in the form of gifts or loans.

The amount of money the Western world gives away every year is so huge that no one can grasp or understand the real magnitude of international aid. Never before in the history of mankind have such enormous sums been extracted from the taxpayers in some countries and transferred to others without any form of compensation or repayment.

International aid is unique in our history. It is the only type of government spending and the only type of government activity over which the citizens, who pay the enormous sums, have neither any direct control nor any firsthand knowledge. The projects are carried out thousands of kilometers away in steaming jungles, remote semideserts, or African villages where it is impossible for the real donors of international aid, the taxpayers, to ascertain whether the projects are successful, or indeed even to find out whether the projects are carried out at all.

The most gigantic apparatus for propaganda and indoctrination the world has ever known, the information departments of the United Nations and the huge international bureaucracy involved with aid to Africa and the rest of the Third World, is so effective that, in the relatively short period of ten to twenty years, the citizens of the U.S. and the countries of Europe have been brainwashed into accepting that they will forever work without compensation to promote "development" in some remote part of the world.

Without this overwhelming amount of propaganda and indoctrination, it would be difficult to convince small countries in Europe with no guilt-complex from a colonial past, like Norway, Sweden, and Denmark, that they should contribute enormous sums to foreign aid. So huge is the contribution to foreign aid from small countries such as Norway that it requires a work force of 100,000 men to work for about a year to provide the tax money that enables Norway to spend annually more than 3.6 billion Norwegian kroner on international aid projects.

Since we, the taxpayers, pay for the enormous sums that every year disappear in the African continent and other exotic parts of the world, we should have the right to know *exactly* how the money is spent. Since it concerns us all, we should also demand to know if our foreign aid is successful or not.

The citizens of the countries of Europe and North America are kept informed all right, but not in a way they really want or can really accept. They are kept informed not by some unbiased organization or independent economist, sociologist, or scientist who is an expert on Africa but by the very organizations that spend their tax money overseas.

This principle is fundamentally wrong, but nevertheless the huge international bureaucracy, the United Nations, and all the national aid organizations spend millions—in a small country like Norway, about 11 million kroner —every year on what they call information to justify their current spending and the ever increasing request for more funds to waste in Africa and elsewhere.

In spite of the fact that Africa and most of the Third World is worse off after thirty years of independence from colonial rule and after more than twenty years of international aid, the myth is kept alive that aid does work. The international and national bureaucracy, which forms the nucleus of all international aid, is caught in a self-perpetuating vicious circle that demands more money, bigger loans, further food supplies, and an increasing number of aid projects in order to "develop" Africa and the rest of the Third World.

To accept the facts and to publish the truth that the present form of aid is a failure would destroy the jobs of ten thousand of the best-paid bureaucrats the world has ever known. This could be disastrous for their own positions, and for their own sake—not out of consideration for the poor people they would like to help—the international and national aid bureaucrats devote a large part of their time and the huge apparatus of propaganda at their disposal to build up an image of successful aid, which is almost impossible to verify or control.

We do not believe that the present form of international aid is a success, and we are convinced it does not work in Africa. But in spite of all the accumulated proof that international aid is to a large extent a failure—and certainly not a success in relation to the huge amounts of money involved—international and national aid organizations maintain the myth that as long as we give more and more money away, foreign aid will eventually be a success.

Rarely do aid organizations present a true picture of the impact of aid on Africa. On the contrary, the true results after twenty years of international aid to Africa are covered up by the most extensive, elaborate, and costly deceit ever to occur in history. What is most ironic, and also most tragic, is that it is paid for by the victims of the fraud —taxpayers. The results are not what we find in colorful publications, glossy photographs, propaganda films, and radio programs prepared by international and national aid organizations. What foreign aid has done to Africa is quite different. It is a grim story of the devastating effect of attempting to compress the development of a continent into a few years of forcing Africans into cultural, economic, and political systems that do not work because they are foreign and alien to the continent.

Most international aid to Africa is fundamentally wrong, not because the projects are wasted or of no lasting value, which they often are, but because international aid creates serious problems for developing countries that would have been unknown if international aid did not exist.

If Africa had been left to herself, the growth of the population would have been in relation to the continent's ability to produce food. The population would have grown only as fast as food production permitted, and the natural equilibrium would have been maintained. By destroying the natural equilibrium between man and nature in Africa, international and national aid organizations have provided the conditions for the most devastating catastrophe any continent has been exposed to: the doubling of its population by the year 2000.

Even more disastrous than the doubling of the total population in about twenty years is the huge migration from the countryside to the enormous slums of Africa's cities. Through international aid, we have destroyed the indigenous culture and economy. Uprooting millions, we have created monster cities and wrecked African tribal and social systems. We have created an apathy among the Africans, reduced their initiative to help themselves and forced the Africans to be more dependent upon Europe and the U.S.—even more dependent than they were under colonial rule.

There is no country in Africa today which can document

genuine progress and development irrespective of what political or economic system they have tried. All options have proved to be a failure, whether it is African socialism in Tanzania, Soviet-style Marxism in Mozambique, a moderate free-enterprise system in Kenya, or supercapitalism in oil-rich Nigeria. Whether it comes from the billions provided by international aid or from the huge oil revenues in Nigeria, money has brought only failure.

While international aid has created the conditions for the disastrous population explosion, it is unable to solve the most elementary problem of a genuine development of the continent because

- too much money is spread over a large number of small projects that have little or no lasting value,
- huge sums of money are spent on projects the Africans are fully capable of carrying out themselves,
- small-scale industries and so-called appropriate technology that in the long run contribute little to real development are encouraged and supported, and
- the wrong type of agriculture—either primitive small-scale farming or huge state-owned enterprises—is encouraged and supported, neither of which will provide Africa with the extra food it so desperately needs.

The Africans themselves know that the present form of aid does not work, as the following statements of high-ranking black officials clearly demonstrate:

The agricultural self-sufficiency of Africa will decline from 90 per cent in 1980 to 60 per cent in the year 2000, while there at the same time will be 17 million unemployed. It is clear that if we don't change our way of development and our conception of development, we will be destroyed" (Edem Kodjo, secretary-general of the OAU, Johannesburg *Sunday Times*, September 14, 1980).

On the basis of all the economic projections we have seen so far, Africa in the year 2000 will not be in the ditch it is in now. It will be in the bottom of a deep black hole" (A senior official of the UN

Economic Commission for Africa, OECD *Observer*, January 1981).

Everything has deteriorated, and the final catastrophe of frightening dimensions is looming on the horizon. International aid has had twenty years to improve the conditions and to prove itself, but instead has only documented that aid is no answer to Africa's problems.

The total accomplishment over this period is disappointing, and everything seems to have gone wrong—so wrong, in fact, that there is doubt that anyone can find a solution before it is too late.

Africa developed for thousands of years in harmony with nature and in equilibrium with its environment. From the day, almost five hundred years ago, when Bartholomew Diaz put his feet on African soil until the last colonial powers left Africa after the Second World War, the continent was changed dramatically. But even during the colonial interlude, the Africans were left to themselves, and they developed according to their ability and desire for progress.

Only when the international and national aid organizations invaded Africa en masse and started their disastrous experiments in foreign aid, was the natural development of Africa disrupted. The result is a catastrophe of which we have seen only the beginning. To the problems international aid has created in Africa, there might be no solution.

Appendix 1

OFFICIAL DEVELOPMENT ASSISTANCE
FROM SIX EUROPEAN AND TWO NORTH AMERICAN
DONOR COUNTRIES

	PERCENT OF GROSS NATIONAL PRODUCTS			
Country	*1977*	*1978*	*1979*	*1980*
Germany	0.33	0.37	0.44	0.43
United Kingdom	0.46	0.48	0.52	0.34
Sweden	0.99	0.90	0.94	0.76
Norway	0.83	0.90	0.93	0.82
Denmark	0.60	0.75	0.75	0.72
Netherland	0.86	0.82	0.93	0.99
U.S.	0.25	0.27	0.19	0.27
Canada	0.48	0.52	0.47	0.42

SOURCE: *World Development Report 1981*, The World Bank, Washington, D.C., 1980. Data are estimates.

Appendix 2

GROWTH RATE AND TOTAL POPULATION OF
SIX DONOR COUNTRIES IN EUROPE AND
SIX RECIPIENT COUNTRIES IN AFRICA

Country	Population in millions	Growth rate in percent
Germany	61.418	0.2
United Kingdom	55.932	0.1
Sweden	8.263	0.4
Norway	4.034	0.6
Denmark	5.076	0.4
The Netherlands	13.864	0.9

SOURCE: *1979 World Bank Atlas*, Washington, D.C.

Country	Population in millions	Growth rate in percent
Kenya	14.614	3.8
Tanzania	16.363	3.0
Zambia	5.128	3.0
Uganda	12.049	3.0
Ghana	10.634	3.0
Zimbabwe	6.683	3.3

SOURCE: *1979 World Bank Atlas*, Washington, D.C.

Appendix 3

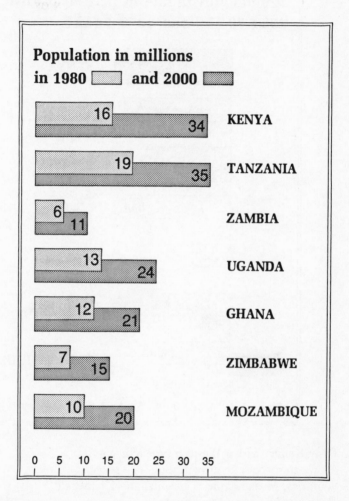

To maintain aid at the same rate as the growth in population will be an impossible task.

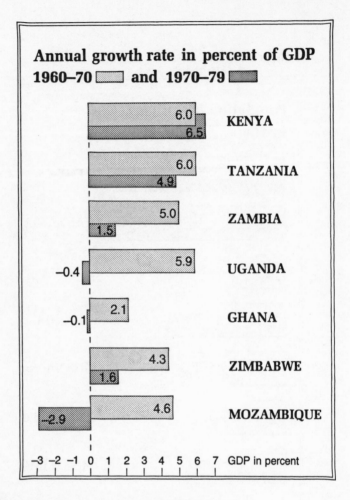

Annual growth rate in percent of GDP
1960–70 ☐ and 1970–79 ▨

6.0 / 6.5	KENYA
6.0 / 4.9	TANZANIA
5.0 / 1.5	ZAMBIA
−0.4 / 5.9	UGANDA
−0.1 / 2.1	GHANA
4.3 / 1.6	ZIMBABWE
4.6 / −2.9	MOZAMBIQUE

−3 −2 −1 0 1 2 3 4 5 6 7 GDP in percent

Only Kenya, with a Western type of economy,
shows an increase in growth rate. The socialist
countries, Mozambique, Tanzania, and Ghana, all
show a reduction in growth rate.

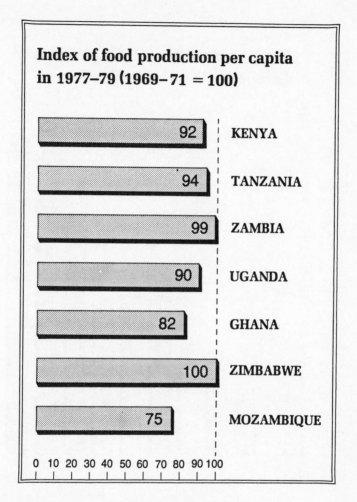

Index of food production per capita in 1977–79 (1969–71 = 100)

92	KENYA
94	TANZANIA
99	ZAMBIA
90	UGANDA
82	GHANA
100	ZIMBABWE
75	MOZAMBIQUE

0 10 20 30 40 50 60 70 80 90 100

All countries that received large amounts of international aid showed a decrease in food production compared with Zimbabwe, which was even exposed to an international blockade.

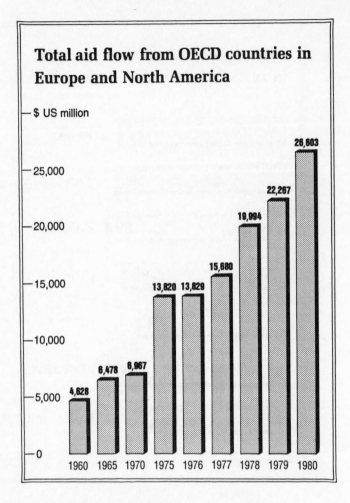

Total aid flow from OECD countries in Europe and North America

$ US million

Year	Value
1960	4,628
1965	6,478
1970	6,967
1975	13,820
1976	13,829
1977	15,680
1978	19,994
1979	22,267
1980	26,603

During the last ten years, total international aid has almost quadrupled while the growth rate of aid recipients in Africa has decreased.

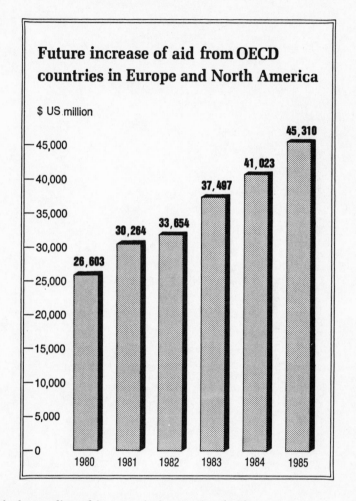

Future increase of aid from OECD countries in Europe and North America

$ US million

1980	26,603
1981	30,264
1982	33,654
1983	37,497
1984	41,023
1985	45,310

With the predicated increase in international aid, the amount for 1985 will be six and a half times greater than in 1970. This tremendously increased aid will be given even though there are few indications that any of it contributes to a genuine development.